MW00777478

THERE IS

SOMETHING STRANGE
ABOUT MY BRAIN

There's Something Strange About My Brain: Writing Horror for Kids is published under Erudition, a sectionalized division under Di Angelo Publications, Inc.

Erudition

Erudition is an imprint of Di Angelo Publications.
Copyright 2023.
All rights reserved.
Printed in the United States of America.

Di Angelo Publications
www.dapbooks.shop

Library of Congress
There's Something Strange About My Brain: Writing Horror for Kids
ISBN: 978-1-955690-53-9
Paperback

Words: R. L. Stine
Cover Photographer: Matt Peyton
Hair and Make-up: Laura Koski
Assistant/Social Manager: Madison Collins
Cover Design: Savina Mayeur
Interior Design: Kimberly James
Editors: Willy Rowberry, Shelly Romero

Downloadable via www.dapbooks.shop and other e-book retailers.

No part of this publication may be reproduced, distributed, or transmitted in any form or by any means without the prior written permission of the publisher, except in the case of brief quotations embodied in critical reviews and certain other noncommercial uses permitted by copyright law. For permission requests, contact info@diangelopublications.com.

For educational, business, and bulk orders, contact distribution@diangelopublications.com.

1. Language Arts & Disciplines --- Writing ---
Children's & Young Adult

THERE IS

SOMETHING STRANGE ABOUT MY BRAIN

WRITING HORROR FOR KIDS

R. L. STINE

Best-Selling author of *Goosebumps* and *Fear Street*

As seen on Masterclass

MasterClass

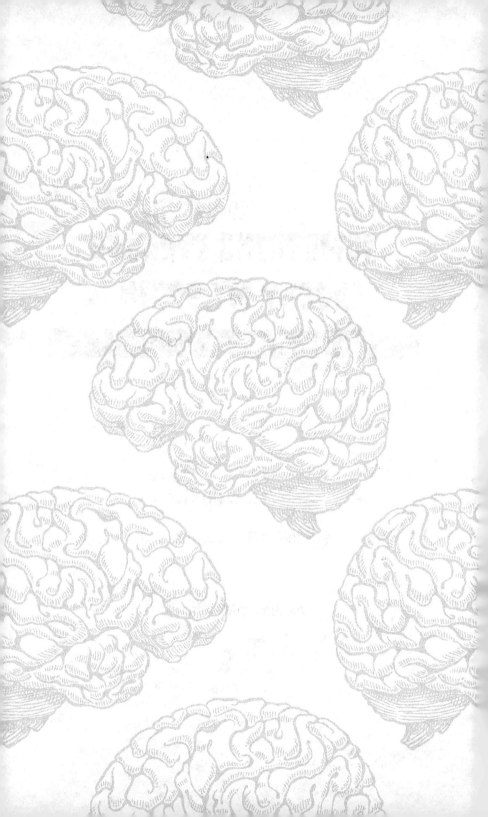

CONTENTS

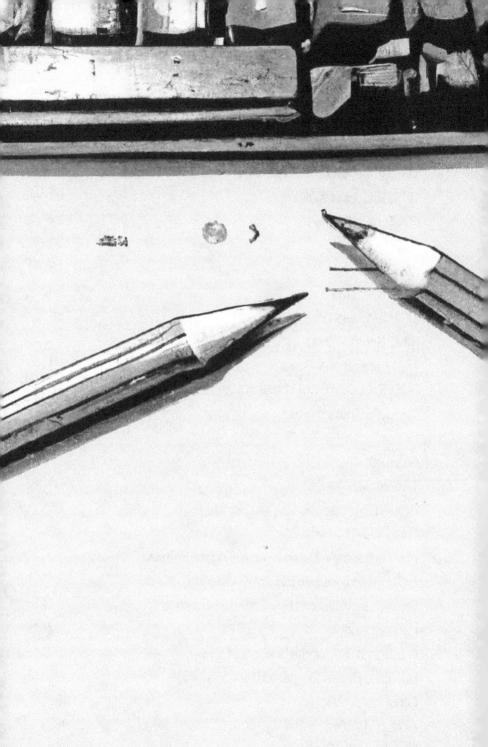

INTRODUCTION

So you think you want to write for young people?

Why?

§ To make some fast bucks?

§ To become famous?

§ To see your ideas turned into movies?

If you answered yes to any of the above, I guess my best advice is to keep your day job.

Let me just tell you that I wrote for twenty years before anyone noticed. And it took twenty-three years for people to want to make a movie about my Goosebumps series.

If your answer to the question is: I have this urge to write that I can't explain. Or: I've always loved to write, and I would really like to entertain young people. Or: I don't know . . .

Then you've probably come to the right place.

I've written more than 350 books, and I can't really tell you why. I always say it's greed and stupidity. But that's just me trying to be funny. What I do know is that the hours I spend writing are the best part of my day.

Maybe I can help you get started writing. Or maybe I can help you enjoy your writing more.

I've put together 62 tips and tricks — all of my writing secrets.

Well, I guess they're not secrets anymore.

I hope these tips inspire you and help you with your writing career.

Wishing you all good luck.

CHAPTER ONE
GET GOING!

Can you really count up all the tips and tricks for becoming a good writer?

I've thought a lot about writing, but I've never tried to count my tricks before — they came out to the strange number of 62 — so this was a new experience for me, as it will be for you.

Out of the 62 tips in this book, I hope you find a few bits of advice that will actually spark your imagination and help to inspire your writing.

My first piece of advice is **never be satisfied with your first draft.**

When I started to write this first chapter, these are the first tips I wrote:

1. Before you begin, sharpen five or six #2 pencils and place them near your keyboard

2. That way, if the writing doesn't go well, you can stab yourself in the eyes with them.

After a while, I decided that might be a tiny bit too negative. So I tossed out the first draft and began again.

Well . . . let's GET GOING.

1. STAY AWAY FROM THE FREEZER!

When I was a kid, we had a meat freezer in the basement of our house — a big white enamel monstrosity shaped like a coffin. Every time I had to go down to get something from it, my mind raced with terrifying possibilities: What if I found a frozen corpse inside? What if I leaned down too far, fell inside, and the lid slammed shut on me? I didn't know it, but I was already dreaming up horror plots.

Sure enough, one day my dad asked me to bring up a roast beef. I went down to the basement, lifted the wide lid of the freezer, and gasped in horror. The frozen blue corpse of a young man lay stretched the length of the freezer, glassy eyes staring up at me.

I let out a shrill cry. The freezer lid fell from my hands and—

Oops. Sorry. Sometimes my imagination runs away with me. You didn't believe me, did you? You didn't really believe I found a corpse in my freezer. Of course you didn't.

I'm just saying I had a lot of fears as a kid.

Later, I learned to channel those fears in my writing. I found that the things that scare us the most can often be the source of our greatest inspiration. So if you're like I was, don't let that hold you back. Use your fears to fuel your writing.

2. DO YOU HAVE A COMPULSION? HOW LONG CAN YOU GO WITHOUT WRITING?

If you want to be a writer, you have to be driven to write. It should be a compulsion.

Even though that's my belief, there are a lot of really successful authors who would totally disagree with me. For example, the great thriller writer Harlan Coben is a friend of mine. Harlan and I never talk about writing when we're together. But one evening, Harlan and I did an event at a Barnes & Noble in New York City where we talked about writing, and in that conversation, we discovered that we have nothing in common at all.

I sit down every day. I love to write and write every morning. Harlan has to force himself to write. He has to scream at himself. He has to call himself all kinds of names to get himself to write. I have an office. I have a room in my apartment where I work. Harlan can't work at home. He has to go out to a coffee shop somewhere. He has to be out with people. I like quiet. Harlan has to have music going. I outline every book I write, chapter by chapter. Harlan never plans, never does an outline. Never.

So what does that mean?

Every writer is different. I can only tell you what works for me.

3. BE A READER.

To be a writer, you must first be a reader. It's a natural progression, really. I have found that the more I read, particularly in the genres of thrillers and mysteries, the more it helps my own writing. You observe the way people write, how they craft sentences and stories, and you absorb it.

I make a point to read daily, scouring through new works of fiction, mysteries, and thrillers. In college, as an English major, I was exposed to all the greats, and their works have stayed with me over the years. Don't be afraid to draw inspiration from the books you have loved, to borrow and develop them in your own unique way.

4. DO YOU LIKE IT OR LOVE IT?

If you want to be a writer, you have to actually *like* to write. Of course, that is just the first step. You also need to have a good understanding of the craft. You need to learn how to structure a story, how to create compelling characters, how to use dialogue effectively, and so on. There's a lot to learn, and it can be overwhelming at first.

But if you truly love writing, you'll find that the process of learning how to write is rewarding in itself. You'll know that every word you write is bringing you closer to your goal of becoming a published author.

If you think you want to do it because you want to be famous, or you want your books to become movies, that's probably not a good idea. Things seldom go that way. But many authors get to experience the joy of walking into a bookstore and seeing their title on one of the shelves.

5. WHY DO YOU WANT TO WRITE?

I think that very early on, you have to decide what kind of writer you want to be. I started out writing funny books, and then the scary books came along. My whole goal was to entertain, to get kids to read. I had no further ambition than that.

People always ask, "What are the morals that you're teaching?" There aren't any. In *Goosebumps* or *Fear Street*, there's nothing you can learn except the fun of reading.

Some people think when it comes to kids' books, the kids have to be elevated by what they read. There was always a rule in children's publishing: The characters in a children's book had to learn and grow. I just rejected that idea. I thought if adults can read something with no socially redeeming value whatsoever — just for fun — then kids have the same right.

Authors also come into school and tell kids they have to write from their heart, and I think that's garbage, too.

I've written over 300 books, and I can honestly say that I haven't written a single one from my heart. That's not to say that I don't put my heart into my writing — because I do. But I write for my readers. I write to entertain and make them laugh. I write to get kids to read. That's my passion. And that's what I want to teach you in this book.

6. CHOOSE YOUR GENRE AND AUDIENCE.

Before you start thinking about your audience and who they are, you want to decide what you want to write.

§ What are you interested in?

§ What do you read?

§ Do you read a lot of science fiction?

§ Do you read a lot of romances?

§ Do you find those really fun?

If so, maybe you want to try to write one.

Then once you figure out what genre you want to write, you can start thinking about the audience. Ask questions to figure out what you want to do.

§   Do you want to write for adults? Kids?

§   Do you want to write for a big general audience?

§   Do you want to write for a literary audience?

7. KNOW YOUR MARKET.

Once you've figured out your genre, go to the bookstores or search online to see what's already there. It's important to know the market first — to know what people are reading and where your book will go in the store. Don't try to do something that won't fit in somewhere specific. That almost never works.

I think a lot of people would probably criticize that advice and say, "Don't think about the marketing part first. Just write something you like." But if you write something that no one knows how to market, you're going to have a lot of problems.

8. FIND THE RIGHT DAY JOB.

My very first job was writing for movie magazines. My boss had six magazines that she had to fill every month. And there were three of us writers. We'd come in the morning and she'd say, "Do an interview with Diana Ross." I'd say, "Fine, okay," and make up an interview. Then she'd say, "Do an interview with the Beatles."

That was the job. I would write two or three interviews a day, making up everything. It was actually a very creative job and it was very useful for later on because I learned how to write really fast and I learned how to make up everything.

I went from job to job and eventually ended up at Scholastic, writing for social studies magazines. I'd do my work at Scholastic in the morning, and then I'd do my own writing every afternoon. That might be one reason why they fired me. I don't know. But I'd get my work done quickly so that I could get back to my writing.

It's hard, but if you can find a job that gives you time to write and doesn't take all your energy away, that's certainly what I would recommend.

9. ALWAYS SAY "YES."

Always say "yes" to everything. I wouldn't have this career if I didn't have that policy.

One day I was having lunch with my friend Jean Feiwel, who was the editorial director of Scholastic at the time. And Jean had just had a fight with a writer who wrote YA horror. She sat down to lunch and she said, "I'm never working with him again. You could write a good teen horror novel. Go home and write a book called 'Blind Date.'"

I didn't know what she was talking about. What does that mean? Teen horror novel? I said, "Yes, sure," because

I always say yes. Then I went running to the bookstore and I read Christopher Pike, Lois Duncan, Richie Tankersley Cusick, Diane Hoh, and all these other people who were writing teen horror at the time so I could find out what the genre was.

I wrote Blind Date, and it was a number one bestseller. I was shocked. I'd never been close to a bestseller list. A year later, I wrote a second teen horror book called *Twisted*. Again, a number one bestseller. I thought, *Forget the funny stuff. I'm going to be scary from now on!*

If I had said, "Well, Jean, I don't really know what you're talking about. You know, I'm a funny guy. I write jokes. I don't write horror," I wouldn't have had this amazing career. None of it would have happened.

It all came from saying, "Yes."

CHAPTER TWO

WHAT ABOUT YOUR READERS?

10. UNDERSTAND YOUR AUDIENCE.

I like to know my audience. I want my books to seem real and current to them. I do book signings and visit schools all the time so that I can see who I'm writing for and remember them when I'm writing. I listen to what they say and what expressions they use. I notice what they wear. I try to keep up with their music and what they watch on Netflix. It's very important not to sound like some old guy from Mars who doesn't know anything.

11. DON'T MAKE IT TOO HARD FOR THEM.

I write my middle grade books at a fourth-grade reading level because I'm trying to motivate kids to read. I don't make the reading challenging. I make it inviting.

The reading level is low. There are no hard vocabulary words or new vocabulary words to learn. No difficult concepts or challenges. Short sentences with easy-to-read words within short chapters. There's nothing that could keep them from reading on and on and on.

12. DON'T GO OVER THEIR HEADS.

Middle Grade: Keep in mind these readers are as young as seven.

My big rule for writing middle-grade horror is that the reader has to know it's a fantasy. Horror doesn't have to be traumatizing. It's got to be scary. It's got to be creepy, but I don't want parents to come up to me at a book signing and say, "Your book gave our kid nightmares for weeks. Our kid had to sleep with us." That is not what I want to do at all.

In fact, a woman wrote to me once with the perfect line in the perfect letter. She wrote, "I love your books for my kids because they give them shudders, but not nightmares." And that's what I try to do.

YA Fiction: Make the horror realistic.

I don't believe that violence in books is harmful to young people in any way. There's a very big difference between reading violence and witnessing violence. Teenagers are smart. They can distinguish real-life from fiction. Since they know it's fiction, the scares in YA books can be taken far.

And the older your readers get, the more details they demand. I have to build up the world with real-world images and issues that I wouldn't include in a middle-grade book. The dialogue has to be current and realistic. The characters have to have real problems. Family problems. Kids whose parents are out of work. Maybe the father loses a job. The kids are desperate. Maybe they're thinking about robbing a store or something. Otherwise, the story is just going to be silly to them.

EXPERIENCE

MEMORY

IMAGINATION

CHAPTER THREE

CONCEPTUALIZING

13. YOU ONLY NEED ONE IDEA.

Every author is asked the same question: "Where do you get your ideas?" It's the question that adults ask, kids ask, and reporters ask. It's the question that two-thirds of my fanmail starts with. "Dear R.L. Stine, Our teacher is forcing us to write to an author. I chose you. Where do you get your ideas?"

For a long time, I used to tell students that I got my ideas at the Ideas Store.

The Ideas Store has three departments: Experience, Memory, and Imagination. **Experience** is the things that happen to you in real life — what you see, hear, feel, and do. **Memory** is your recollection of those experiences. It's your ability to recall events, emotions, and sensations. **Imagination** is the ability to take those experiences and memories and twist them into something new, something unexpected, something scary.

I've written over 300 books — one at a time. You only need just one idea to get started.

14. DRAW FROM YOUR OWN EXPERIENCE.

Experience comes from what happens to you in your everyday, real world life. It exists there in the things you see, hear, feel, and do. Whether your experiences are good or bad, explore them.

Keep your eyes and ears open for any ideas that come your way. Shift your awareness to what you can sense in your day-to-day occurrences. You never know when inspiration might strike. You might be walking down the street, or watching a family at the airport, or even just daydreaming in the shower, and suddenly an idea will come to you. That's why it's essential to always be alert and open to the world around you. Who knows what kind of stories you might discover?

15. GET IDEAS FROM YOUR MEMORY.

Memory is your recollection of events, emotions, and sensations. Dig deep into your memories, and remember the things that made you happy, sad, or scared. Think back to things that will give you some kind of spark.

As kids, my brother and I used to worry about our parents coming home late. We would wait anxiously, wondering where they were and if they were okay. Many years later, that memory sparked an idea. What if they *never* came back? That thought became the inspiration for one of my first *Fear Street* books, *Missing*. Even something as mundane as my father's ugly lawn gnomes that he loved so much became the inspiration for one of my *Goosebumps* books, *Attack of the Lawn Gnomes*.

16. USE YOUR IMAGINATION TO GENERATE IDEAS.

As an author, you're going to use your imagination more than anything else. Imagination is the ability to take your experiences and memories and twist them into something new.

When I was young, I was very fearful. I was afraid of the dark, afraid of the basement, afraid of big dogs . . . It was a terrible way to be a kid. But later, when I started writing scary novels, the memory of those fears came in handy and I turned them into stories.

Nothing is scarier than your imagination fueling your fears, so use that.

17. THINK OF TITLES INSTEAD OF IDEAS.

A good title will lead you to the idea for the story. It establishes the tone and nature of the book, attracting the reader and revealing what will be in store for them. I wrote a *Fear Street* book called *Give Me a K. I. L. L.* Right from the start, you know it's a cheerleader book and you know someone's going to die.

Once, I was walking my dog in Riverside Park in New York when the words "Say cheese and die" just popped into my head. It was like a lightning bolt hit me. I started to think about it and wonder, "What if there was an evil camera?" That's when the idea for one of my most popular *Goosebumps* books was born.

The title for my *Mostly Ghostly* series came from a sign I read while I was at a Wal-Mart during Halloween time. These ideas can come from anywhere and at any time.

A great and important way to get inspiration for titles is from all the things that you read, watch, and love.

When we were kids, my brother and I used to go see a horror movie every Saturday afternoon. We saw all the classic horror films: *20,000 Fathoms, The Creature from the Black Lagoon, It Walks Among Us, The Brain That Wouldn't Die, It Came From Beneath the Sea.* I've since borrowed germs of ideas from those great titles.

CHAPTER FOUR

DEVELOPMENT

18. CREATE A RELATABLE CHARACTER.

When you start to write, you want to create a protagonist that readers are going to relate to or want to root for throughout a whole book.

When I write a *Goosebumps* book and I'm figuring out the characters, I don't delve too deeply into the details of who they are. I give them a little description. The kids in *Goosebumps* are always normal kids. Sometimes they play an instrument or something, but they're not special in any way. They can get into more trouble this way. And they're always 12 because the readers are a little bit younger and they like to read about kids who are older.

So, we have these ordinary kids in extraordinary circumstances solving this problem, trying to get out of danger, saving their lives on their own with their own smarts and their own imagination. And you want the reader to identify with them and become part of the book, to experience what the protagonist is experiencing. And that it makes it more scary.

19. MAKE YOUR YA CHARACTER FEEL LIKE A REAL TEENAGER.

To me, a lot of teen fiction is too grim. No one ever cracks a joke. No one's ever laughing about anything. I don't know why. You need that in the book. It's more true to life. When you observe a bunch of teenagers, they're laughing all the time and they're having fun.

You have to know what these characters want, what their goal is. You want to develop characters that aren't cliches, but there are still archetypes they fall into.

For example: you have a guy who's very angry and his household is a mess and he wants to drop out. That creates a lot of tension immediately and shows the readers what the stakes are for this character.

20. CHOOSE RELATABLE NAMES.

Back when we were starting *Goosebumps* in the '90s, I had my son's school directory and I used it as a reference because I needed a lot of names. I think I used every kid at his school in the *Goosebumps* books. Sometimes my son would come home and he'd say, "Dad, you have to put Jamie in the next one." Or, "Dad, you have to use Will." It turns out the kids had paid him ten bucks to be in the next book.

Now, I try to find names online that are really popular and are current. You can easily search for the twenty most popular names for boys and girls, because then more kids will be able to identify with them. And be sure to use a wide range of names reflecting a wide range of ethnic diversity. We are in a great age of inclusivity.

21. KEEP IT REAL

Always think back to the age group that's talking.

Kids don't speak in complete sentences. I don't know any kids who talk in full sentences. Teenage guys mostly grunt. When you have to create dialogue, remember, kids don't speak in really long sentences with difficult words, so it's fine to include sentence fragments or very short sentences with a low vocabulary level when you have kids talking.

YA Character Cheat Sheet

When I'm planning any book, I make a cheat sheet of most of the main characters with their traits and what they look like. I don't do it for every single one. Some I improvise as I'm writing the book. This is the one I wrote when I was planning out the Fear Street book, *Give Me a K. I. L L.*

Character Cheat Sheet

GIVE ME A K-I-L-L

Gretchen Page
- *Straight blonde hair—olive-colored eyes*
- *White*
- *Not happy with her looks*
- *Nose too short—hates the cleft in her chin*
- *Tense—has nightmares*
- *Small-town girl, Shadyside High is big to her*
- *Uncomfortable in new school*
- *Ambitious*
- *Determined to win*

Gretchen's Mom
- *Tall, athletic*
- *White*
- *Short blonde hair streaked with white*
- *Young-looking for 43*
- *Haggard since her divorce*
- *Wears too much makeup, Gretchen thinks*

Coach Walker
- *Cheerleader coach*
- *Very tall and thin*
- *Black*
- *All business but sympathetic*
- *Very fair-minded and reasonable*
- *Not afraid to stand up to Devra*

Devra Dalby

- *Rich, cold, snobbish*
- *Blue eyes, wavy red hair*
- *Creamy white skin*
- *Beautiful but icy*
- *Cutting sense of humor*
- *Totally entitled*
- *Father owns dept. store chain*

Madison Grossman

- *Plays violin (since she was three)*
- *Very pale*
- *Intense*
- *Very thin, birdlike*
- *Long curly black hair*
- *Sharp nose*
- *Very tightly wired*
- *Artistic family*

Sid Viviano

- *Sense of humor, funny*
- *Wears a lot of denim*
- *Serious dark eyes that crinkle up when he smiles*
- *White*
- *Short brown hair, buzzed haircut*
- *Warm and likable*
- *Good looking except for big ears*

So I had a pretty good idea of Gretchen. She's the main character in the book. She was moving from a small town that was even smaller than Shadyside. I had the tension come from the move and the problems that can cause teenagers. Devra Dalby is related to a character from the old days in Silent Night (Fear Street: Super Chillers), where her cousin was the same type of spoiled, rich teenager.

Try your hand at it. It doesn't need to be detailed, but you should be able to get an idea of the characters, what they look like, and what their personalities are.

CHAPTER FIVE

PLOTTING

22. START WITH A LOCATION OR EVENT.

Setting up a familiar scene helps readers connect with your story. If it is not something that's a part of their lives, they'll have trouble imagining it. That's why most Goosebumps books take place in backyards, schools, basements, and summer camps. Take a normal place and input something scary.

23. START WITH A MONSTER—AND ANYTHING CAN BE A MONSTER.

What makes a monster a monster? For me, it's anything that cannot be controlled. I believe one reason kids like *Goosebumps* is that they identify with the monsters—not the protagonist. I think they identify with these raging creatures because sometimes kids feel out of control and angry. Sometimes they're anxious. They have to suppress these feelings and hold them in. A monster, however, is something that doesn't suppress emotions at all.

Take any inanimate but familiar object and make it terrible, give it power. Have it do horrible things. Any time you take an inanimate object, especially something that's almost human and you give it qualities like the ability to move and create a sound — I think that's very terrifying. Of all the creatures I've created, Slappy has been the one that's really captured everyone's imagination. The idea of a doll coming to life is very scary to a lot of people.

What could *you* bring to life?

24. START STRONG AND SET UP THE ACTION IMMEDIATELY.

Within the first chapter, readers should have an idea of the central conflict — what the problem is and what's going to develop. You've got to get the characters in, get them described, and then get into the action. There's no time for background. Nothing should interfere with the action and the narrative momentum. Waiting too long to give this information risks losing your reader's attention before they've read far enough.

I once wrote an outline for *I am Slapppy's Evil Twin,* which was rejected by my editors (*ref. back matter*). In this first outline, Slappy didn't appear until Chapter 13, and that was a real problem. The editors said, "How can you do a Slappy book when he isn't there? He doesn't even appear till nearly two thirds of the way through the book." I was trying something a little different, but they hated it. In my revised version, Slappy and his twin both appear in chapter one. Because of that, the book gets off to a really fast start.

Slappy's Evil Twin
First Chapter Case Study

I'll use *I Am Slappy's Evil Twin* because I think it's a really good example of what you want to do in the first chapter. You want to meet the kids. You want to kind of find out what they're like. And then you want to know what's going to happen right away. This chapter pretty much does that.

"Hey, guys. I'm Luke Harrison. I'm the redheaded kid poking around in the tool chest in the garage, trying to figure out what a Phillips screwdriver looks like. Yes, I'm 12."

As are all Goosebumps kids.

"I probably should know more about tools by now. But I'm not the mechanical type. I mean, the most complicated thing I ever built was a snowman! That's a joke. Actually, I've never built anything in my life--until we decided to build this drone for a school contest"

Luke is the main character and you know quite a bit about him just in the first two paragraphs.

"'Hurry up, Luke. I can't hold this forever.'

"That's my sister, Kelly, across the garage. She's holding two pieces of the frame together. Kelly isn't much help either. Well...she's good at holding things. And she's good at telling us what we're doing wrong. So I guess that's helpful."

Now we know Kelly, Luke's sister.

"Luckily, our friend Jamal is a mechanical genius. No. Seriously. He's a genius with this stuff. He was one of those kids who built an entire city as big as his living room out of LEGOs when he was still in diapers. Jamal bought the "Make-Your-Own-Drone: kit we're using. And when he spread all the pieces out in our garage, he didn't like the instructions. So he threw them out. He said he could do it better. And we believed him."

And Jamal.

Now onto the chapter ending.

"The drone had four motors. We had special batteries for the motors. And then a small propane tank for the back of the frame. I guess for liftoff. Kelly and Jamal began to assemble another side of the frame. The afternoon sun slid behind some trees and shadows swept over the garage. I stepped to the back wall and clicked on the garage lights.

"'Don't say I'm not helpful,' I called to them. They ignored me. I turned and stumbled over the big propane tank. The tank was huge, about three feet taller than me. It looked like the water heater we have in the basement. I stumbled into it, and as I watched in horror, the tank began to tilt and fall over. I made a wild grab for it, but it was too heavy. It slipped right out of my hands. Like a nightmare, the whole thing seemed to be happening in slow motion. The tank was going down, about to crash onto the hard concrete floor. I grabbed for it again. Missed. And then I screamed. 'Look out. It's going to BLOW!'"

End of chapter 4.

In this first chapter from Luke's POV, you can see that we've established the characters and their personalities very quickly, we've started the action right away, and we've introduced a propane tank.

Since I've already planned the ending, I had to establish the presence of the propane tank right away. Of course, the tank doesn't blow up right after this. But we now know it's there and it's there because it plays a major role in the end of the book.

25. USE CLIFFHANGERS.

Make the readers ask, "What happens next?" Every chapter in my books has a cliffhanger ending. Is the character going to survive? Will they make it? You have to go on to the next chapter. My idea is to get kids reading and to keep them reading.

For me, these cliffhanger chapter endings are just as important as anything else in the book. It's a matter of leaving the reader in suspense and having them want to go on and read the next chapter.

Cliffhanger Case Study: *The Haunted Mask*

I think *The Haunted Mask* is my best Halloween story out of all of them. Here is a very typical cliffhanger. It's a very cheap trick that I've probably used in a hundred different chapters.

Carly Beth is wearing the haunted mask. It's stuck to her face and it's turned her really evil and she can't do anything about it. And now she's done something to her friends, and now she's running ... running wildly over the front lawns, jumping over shrubs and hedges, flying over the dark, hard ground. She's running blindly, the houses whirring past on both sides. Carly Beth is out of control now.

"The blustery wind swirled, and she swirled with it, rising over the sidewalks, rushing through tall weeds blowing with the wind like a helpless leaf. Holding her bulging candy bag, she ran past startled trick-or-treaters, past glowing pumpkins, past rattling skeletons. She ran until her breath gave out. Then she stopped, panting loudly, and shut her eyes, waiting for her heart to stop pounding, for the blood to stop pulsing at her temples. And a hand grabbed her shoulder roughly from behind."

And that's the chapter ending. Who grabbed her from behind? Why? You feel Carly Beth's panic here which is out of control, blowing like a leaf in the wind and then something grabs her. But it turns out to be her best friend, Sabrina. It's a tease. It's not a real scare. About half the cliffhangers I use are teasers, and the other half are real scares.

26. INCLUDE A TWIST.

There was one great line in the *Goosebumps* movie that I really loved. Jack Black plays me and at the end of the movie, he's a teacher. He tells his class, "Every story ever told can be broken down into three distinct parts: the beginning, the middle, and the twist." I just think that's great!

The key to your twist is making sure it doesn't come too soon and that it isn't predictable from the start. It's very important to mislead your readers. Don't leave clues to the surprises that are coming. I don't want readers to guess.

Sometimes I'll write an outline and put what I think is a surprising twist in the middle of the book. But then my outline comes back from my editors and they say, "Oh, we guessed that already back in chapter two, you got to work on that." It's hard because I've got to come up with a way to keep that same twist, go back to the beginning, and figure out how to hide it and not make it obvious to the reader.

But if you figure out how to effectively pull off a twist, the whole book is suddenly turned around and no one is who the reader thought they were. I try to have major twists and surprises in every book. It's my favorite part of Goosebumps.

27. DON'T DATE YOUR BOOKS INTO OBSOLETION.

Pop culture, slang, and technology change constantly, so you have to be very careful and try to avoid specific references. You don't want readers to be confused or bored if they pick up your book and don't understand the references. You want to keep readers engaged.

I happened to be looking at a *Fear Street* book the other day and I read the words, "Oh, we're going to a Rick Astley concert." I thought, "Who is that? What was I thinking?" Maybe in 1990 Rick Astley was in, right? And now here he is in this book thirty years later and it's irrelevant because Rick Astley is now mainly obscurely known for Rickrolling. It's a horrible mistake.

28. DON'T LET TECHNOLOGY RUIN YOUR PLOT.

Get rid of technology in your story or try to make it useless. Cell phones have ruined just about every mystery plot. And this is a real problem for writers who want to write mysteries or horror.

In the old days, I would write a *Fear Street* plot where a teenage girl is getting threatening phone calls and she doesn't know who it is or how to ask for help. Now if we've got kids trapped in a cabin in the woods with a murderer, they can pick up their phones, find a signal, and call for help.

One way I worked through this issue was in a new *Fear Street* book called *Party Games* where one of the kids has a birthday party on Fear Island and invites everyone to his summer house in the winter. They're on this deserted island and the very first thing the host does when they arrive is collect all the cell phones.

29. GET YOUR PROTAGONIST INTO LOTS OF TROUBLE.

When you're writing horror, thrillers, mysteries, have to remember that you are actually the enemy of the protagonist. This is a very important thing. You have to cause all kinds of problems throughout the book for your protagonist and then finally get them out in the end. The more trouble you get your protagonist in, the tighter the net you wrap around them, the more fun the book will be and the more satisfying your ending will be.

30. THERE HAVE TO BE FUNNY THINGS THAT HAPPEN. FUNNY CONFLICTS.

You need some normal life, some quiet moments, some fun, between the horrifying scenes. You need to strike a balance in a scary book. Not enough scares, and your story is boring. Too many scares and the story becomes ridiculous and not believable.

Don't leave out the humor and the quiet, normal moments.

31. END HAPPY.

Kids will not accept an unhappy ending. Just for fun, I once wrote a *Fear Street* book, *The Best Friend*, and I put an unhappy ending on it. I had never done it before. At the end, the good girl is taken away as a murderer. And the girl who committed the murder gets off scot free. I just did it for fun.

My readers turned on me immediately. And I started getting angry letters right away asking "You moron! How could you do that?" "What were you thinking?" and "Are you going to write a sequel to finish the story?" Everywhere I went, it haunted me. Every time I would go visit schools, someone would raise their hand and ask those same questions and I actually had to write a sequel to put a happy ending on it.

Fear Street and *Goosebumps* readers like a happy ending because they've been through all this trouble with all these monsters and creepy, terrible adventures they've had. They want relief. They expect a good outcome.

CHAPTER SIX

OUTLINING

32. BE IN CONTROL.

In interviews, a lot of authors say, "I wait for my characters to tell me what to do." "Oh, I wait for my characters to tell me which one of them will be the main character, and my characters will tell me the plot." I always think that's garbage. You're the author. Be in control. You're creating this world and creating these people.

33. HAVE NOTES.

If you jump straight into writing the story, you might find that you're lost in your own creation. When this is happening to me, I think of different scenes and details, and I write those things down before writing or outlining. I write all of the brainstorming down, because it's easier to weed out bad ideas than it is to come up with strictly good ideas.

After, I have my notes, then I start to outline. My outlines are usually 15 to 20 pages long and I spend at least a week on one. It may sound like more work, but it saves time in the grand scheme of things.

Outlining is about making sure the story makes sense and making sure that I track the characters all the way through. It helps guarantee that I have good chapter endings, that the surprises are there, and that there's a good middle.

34. START WITH AN ENDING.

If I know the big finish, then when I start writing my outline, I can make sure that I keep the reader from guessing the ending. When I know what the ending is, I can keep the reader away from it. I can deliberately move the reader in a different direction, then move them in this direction and move them in that direction. This helps make the ending a huge surprise.

35. GET FEEDBACK ON YOUR OUTLINE AND REVISE IT.

When you have an outline that you like, it's good to show it to somebody. Now you're going to find out whether it's a good outline or not. A reader will help you with that determination.

Get someone you trust, who likes to read. Have them

comment. Do they think the pacing is right? Do they think there is enough adventure? Is there enough plot in the story to keep people reading? Does it make sense? Are the characters consistent?

Use these notes to improve on what you have. Each time that I revise the outline it gets better. I've done some books where I've done maybe three or four outlines before I started to write. But I could see the book getting better each time. I hate this part, but I see it getting better.

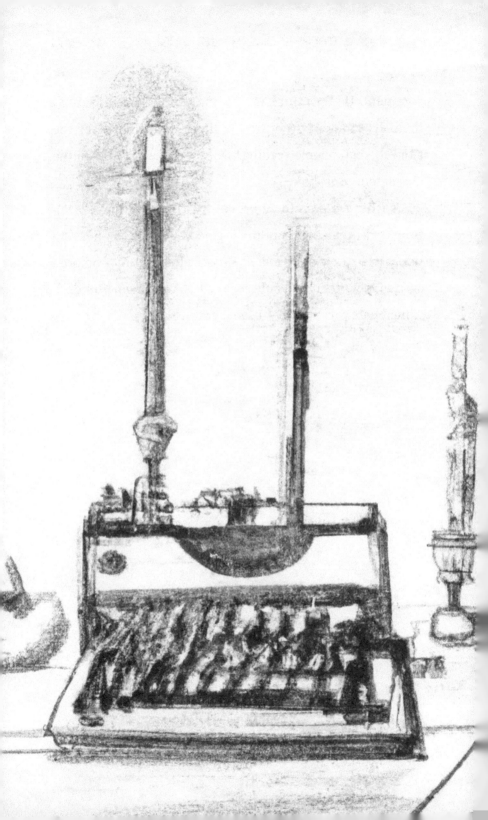

CHAPTER SEVEN

WRITING

36. FIND YOUR TOOLS.

I get a lot of letters from parents now and a lot of tweets saying, "Oh, my son loved the *Goosebumps* movie and they saw you writing on a typewriter. So I had to buy them a typewriter." And they send me pictures and there's a kid there writing on a typewriter.

A typewriter? Really??

It's hard to believe. It's actually very funny. Back in the day, I wrote maybe 100 books on a typewriter. I don't know how. How did anyone revise on a typewriter?

I write all my stories on a Mac desktop, except for my outlines. I have to plot on a yellow pad. Everyone has these kinds of idiosyncrasies. You should try both ways and see which way works for you.

37. CREATE YOUR WRITING ENVIRONMENT.

Every writer has their rituals for their writing environment. I had a friend who wrote Teen Horror back in the '90s and to write, she had to have very creepy music playing, candles lit all over the room, and she wrote on a haunted desk (at least, that's what she claimed).

Personally, I can write anywhere. I used to write on the airplane or in a hotel room. I don't need any special setting but I do need quiet. I can't write with music on.

Find your own rituals and create your perfect environment.

38. DISCIPLINE YOURSELF.

When it comes to writing. It's a good thing to aim for discipline. I'll tell you my routine and I really recommend this––maybe not the hours that I do, but to be able to stick to it every day.

And after 31 years of *Goosebumps,* I sit down at maybe 9:30 in the morning and I start to write. I set a goal for myself every morning: "Today I'm going to write 2,000 words." (*Goosebumps* books have to be around 23,000 words.) And then I don't get up till I've done 2,000 words.

Maybe I'll take 15 minutes to have a sandwich, but then I'm back at it. And when I hit my 2,000 words, I quit. Doesn't matter where I am in the story. It's kind of a trick that I use because when I sit down the next day, I don't have to start all over again. I don't have to do much thinking. I'm in the middle of something already.

39. HAVE FUN WITH THE FIRST DRAFT.

The first draft should be fun and should go fast. Don't think of it as hard work or a struggle. Enjoy everything about what you're doing. Enjoy creating your characters and enjoy making them say all kinds of things. If you're having trouble with the first draft, just keep going. Keep up a steady pace. No matter what, finish your first draft.

When you have a complete draft, you can go back and read it through to see what the problems are, fix up the writing, and take things out that you don't like. Some authors do many drafts before they turn the book in. Don't let worries you have about the first draft slow you down. Just write it. Get the words out.

Remember to enjoy the process. You're not going to turn in the first draft.

40. INTIMIDATED BY WRITING A NOVEL? WRITE A SHORT STORY.

As an aspiring writer, if you feel that it's too ambitious for you to plan a 200-to-300-page novel, try writing a short story.

The short story is a microcosm of the novel. What I find interesting about short stories — and maybe you will too — is that writing short stories is harder because you have to be so concise in a small amount of space.

When I write a short story, I've got to set it up quickly with one really solid idea. I have to figure out who these characters are. I've got to get that characterization completed. I've got to get to the problem right away, and then I have to have a really good ending.

41. WRITE IN CHRONOLOGICAL ORDER.

After the outline is approved, I'm ready to go. I sit down and I start Chapter One. I always write in order. I'm the kind of writer where I have to write from the beginning. I can't skip around. When we were first starting out, my wife and I collaborated on some kids books. We did a book called *The Sick of Being Sick Book* and a couple of others.

It didn't end well because Jane liked to write some of the middle and then go back and write the beginning. I couldn't do that. I probably shouldn't tell this story, but the collaboration actually ended up with her locking me in the closet and leaving the apartment. This is true. She got me out about half an hour later, and that was the last book we ever wrote together.

42. AVOID TOO MUCH INTERNAL MONOLOGUE.

You can write the thoughts of your character, but you have to be careful or you'll overdo it. Too much thinking in a book slows it down. For example, if you write: *Julia, you have to be braver. Go in there. I know I can do it,* you have to also describe what the scare is and what danger she is in while moderating what she's thinking. It's a fine line.

43. MAKE THE PARENTS USELESS.

The kids are on their own. In the *Goosebumps* books, they all have parents, of course, but the parents are totally useless. Either they're not there or they don't believe the kids.

The kids come to them and say, "Mom, Dad, the dummy, it's talking. The dummy came alive."

"Sure. Have a nice time. Go play."

The kids have to use their own wits and their own imagination to get out of trouble. The kids are responsible for themselves. That's pretty much every single book.

44. USE DIALOGUE TO TELL THE STORY.

I would estimate my books are about two thirds dialogue — and that's because writing dialogue is the fun part.

Instead of paragraphs, I use short dialogue to tell the whole story through the characters' speech. You gain an understanding of their mental and moral qualities along with their personalities. The conversation also has to tell you something. It has to reveal something about the characters or it has to reveal something about what's going to happen. A little foreshadowing. So much can be included in dialogue, so utilize it where you can.

45. THE CLOSE RELATIONSHIP BETWEEN HORROR AND HUMOR.

Horror and humor are closely connected. When you scare someone, the person gasps and then laughs. If it was all scary, horror wouldn't be very much fun. It would be exhausting and too terrifying. That's why roller coasters are fun. You go up and you rocket all the way down, screaming. Then there's a pause. There's a nice part where you're lulled into thinking you're safe. Then it happens again. Then you're lulled again. That's so much more fun than if it were just thrill after thrill after thrill.

46. USE YOUR FIVE SENSES TO SET YOUR SCENE AND BUILD SUSPENSE.

In order to create suspense, there has to be something unknown first, something that your character doesn't know and must figure out. What's on the other side of the door? What's that pounding? What are those sounds? What's that scraping on the ceiling?

Get inside that character's head and talk about what they see and not so much what they feel. You don't want to write and say, "Oh, it was the scariest moment of my life." You want to have more sounds . . . more scraping sounds . . . and the sounds are coming closer. You want to write it really slowly. You want to know what that kid feels like with his five senses. His skin is tingling. Maybe his teeth are chattering. What does he smell? What does he hear? What can he see in the darkness? Use details to make a picture for the reader.

My *Goosebumps* book *The Scarecrow Walks at Midnight* is set on a farm. I describe the sounds of these scarecrows rushing through the tall cornstalks during the late fall. Just the sound of these scarecrows moving towards the house builds suspense and creates a really terrifying scene.

Scary Scenes Case Study:
It Came from Beneath the Sink!

Here's a scene in which a little kitchen sponge becomes scary. The sponge is actually a bad luck creature called a Grool. I picked this scene because it shows how you can scare your readers when you slow things down. You create tension by not going fast, by not giving away what you're doing, by not telling them what's going to happen.

Then I heard it.

Whoa-ahhh. Whoa-ahhhh.

Breathing!

Whoa-ahhh. Whoa-ahhhh.

The Grool! But where?

I held my breath and stood completely still. I concentrated really hard, trying to figure out exactly where in the inky blackness the breathing came from.

Whoa-ahhh. Whoa-ahhh.

Somewhere to my right?

I knew I had to walk over there and snatch the Grool. But I was afraid to let go of the ladder. Finally, I decided to count my steps there, find the Grool––then count the same number of steps back to the ladder.

I swallowed hard and let go of the ladder. I stepped into the blackness and started counting.

"One...two...three...four..."

The breathing sounded a little closer.

"Five...six... "

See how I've slowed it all down? I keep you waiting. You have to wait. You're anticipating. You're waiting for the horror.

I stopped. I listened hard.

"Huh?' I cried to myself. "What's that scratching

sound?" Then I saw the eyes. Not the Grool's small, round eyes. Big bright eyes. Several pairs of them. All glowing at me in the dark."

That's the cliffhanger chapter ending. What is it? Then you go on to the next chapter.

The scratching grew louder. The eyes stared up at me.

Yellow eyes. Glowing in the darkness.

I heard a creature scrabble over the floor. Felt something warm and furry brush against my leg.

Were they raccoons? Rats?

I didn't want to know.

Another one brushed against me. They were all starting to scrape around on the sewer floor. They were growing restless.

I forced myself to breathe.

Turned.

And started to run.

Get me out of here! I thought. Get me out of here before they attack!

That passage illustrates, one, the power of darkness. Two, you're right inside his mind so it's a good example of why first-person perspective makes for effective scares. And third, you're using all of the senses: he hears the breathing, then he sees the eyes and he feels something brush his leg.

whoa-ahhh

whoa-ahhh

whoa-ahhh

whoa-ahhh

CHAPTER EIGHT

REVISION

47. TAKE TIME TO ENJOY YOUR ACCOMPLISHMENT.

Look at what you've created. You've written your first draft. That's an amazing accomplishment! You're just in the beginning stages, but there it is . . . you have this thing that you've done. It's wonderful. No matter what trouble you may have drafting later on, you know you can do it.

48. READ IT AGAIN FROM THE BEGINNING.

You have a base here. Now you can build on it. Go back to the very beginning and read it as a reader. Look for scenes that seem to drag or ones that don't go far enough. Look for mistakes. Look for consistency within the characters' names, the weather, and the timeline — all the way through.

49. SEARCH FOR TYPOS.

Typos can come in many forms. It's not just misspelled words, but what if you spelled a character's name in two different ways? Look for errors and be consistent in your writing.

50. GET SOMEONE TO READ IT.

After you've gone through it looking for these things, it's really important to find someone who's willing to read it. Find someone who enjoys reading. Someone whose opinion you trust. A lot of people have readers or they have reader clubs. A lot of writers I know have first readers. Some readers do it for fun or you can hire someone.

After they've read it, here are some questions to ask them:

§ What do you think of the characters?

§ Which characters did you like?

§ Did the setting seem real?

§ Did the characters feel like real people?

§ How is the pacing?

§ Do you think it dragged in some places?

§ What did you think?

§ Was there any place you felt lost?

§ Anything you didn't believe?

§ What did you think of the action?

51. TAKE THE FEEDBACK, THEN REVISE.

Editing is always worth it. I've never had a book come out worse after revision. There are some major authors who refuse to be edited and I won't go into who they are, but their work has really suffered. I notice when a book hasn't gone through revision because the writing isn't as good.

52. DON'T BE SENSITIVE.

My advice to writers is to try not to be sensitive. You must be confident and say, "I like what I wrote. This is what I meant to write." Even if people don't like my books, I do. Perhaps that's my big failing as an author -- I like everything I write. I'm happy with what I've done. I'm not anxious about it. I'm not worried about it. It could be a real failure of mine, but being confident in your writing helps you take the feedback, especially the negative feedback. Being able to take criticism helps make life a lot easier.

CHAPTER NINE

SERIES WRITING

53. TRY YOUR HAND AT DEVELOPING A BOOK SERIES.

If you're interested in writing a series, my advice is to start with a standalone book. If that book is successful, you can consider writing a sequel or continuing the story with new books. The key is to let the series grow organically.

In today's publishing landscape, it can be especially challenging to launch a new series due to competition and market saturation. Publishers are more cautious than ever, and it's tougher for them to commit to more than one book at a time.

When we launched *Goosebumps* in 1992, we were fortunate enough to receive a four-book commitment from Scholastic. This would be almost unheard of today.

54. THINK OF THE TYPE OF SERIES YOU WANT TO WRITE.

When it comes to creating a book series, there are a few different routes you can take. One of the easiest is to have a core cast of characters that appears in every book. By keeping the same characters, an author has the opportunity to develop them over time, and readers can become attached to them, eagerly anticipating their appearances in each new installment.

For *Goosebumps*, I opted for what's known as an anthology series where each book is its own self-contained story, with a different cast of characters, setting, and plot. It's a lot of work, but I enjoy the challenge.

With anthology series, readers can jump in anywhere. They don't have to read the books in a specific order to understand what's going on, and they don't have to keep track of a complex cast of characters.

55. DEVELOP THE RULES OF THE WORLD.

As the creator of the *Goosebumps* universe, I have to admit that it's not like the Marvel Universe. It's not cohesive. Everything is separate. But that's part of the charm, isn't it? It's all wild and unpredictable. Take the *Monster Blood* series, for example. Sometimes the blood is blue, sometimes it's green. I'm not consistent about it across the different books.

But inconsistency aside, there are still some rules I follow when writing my stories. One of them is to never mix ghosts and werewolves. It's a big no-no. You always do one or the other. Mixing them together just doesn't work. My editors always remind me of this. Another rule is to not mix things that don't make sense together. You can't have ghosts and invisible things in the same story. It just won't work.

However, I do love to push the limits and create new monsters and creatures that will send shivers down the spines of my young readers. And sometimes, the rules are meant to be broken. Like with the *HorrorLand* series, where I put different monsters and creatures together to create a truly terrifying theme park. It was a risk, but it paid off. And I think that's what makes Goosebumps so fun and exciting to read. You never know what kind of monster or creature will pop up next.

So, while consistency is important in storytelling, sometimes it's the unpredictable and unexpected that make a story truly memorable.

GOOSEBUMPS ORIGIN STORY

As a writer, I have always loved to scare my readers. I was already doing that successfully with my *Fear Street* series, aimed at young adults. But when my editors suggested a series for 7-to-12-year-olds, I initially hesitated. I didn't want to dilute the success of *Fear Street*, and I wasn't sure I could come up with something that would appeal to a younger audience.

However, my editors persisted, convinced that there was a market for spooky stories that wouldn't give younger readers nightmares. So, I decided to give it a shot. But I told them that I needed to come up with the perfect title before I would consider writing the series.

One day, while reading *TV Guide* magazine, a small advertisement caught my eye. It was for a week of scary movies on Channel 11, and the headline read "Goosebumps Week." I knew immediately that I had found the perfect title for the series. "Goosebumps." It was funny, catchy, and most importantly, it conveyed the shivers that I wanted my young readers to feel.

I was excited to get started on *Goosebumps*, but I was still worried about how my young readers would react to my stories. After all, writing for a younger audience was a completely new experience for me.

But as soon as the first book in the series was published, I knew that I had made the right decision. *Goosebumps* became an instant hit, captivating young readers with its mix of humor and fright. I was thrilled to see how much my young readers enjoyed my stories, and the feedback I received from them was incredibly encouraging.

Now, looking back on the last thirty years, it's amazing to see how far the *Goosebumps* series has come. It's been adapted into a successful TV series, a movie franchise, and even video games. But the most rewarding part has been knowing that I've helped introduce a new generation of readers to the joys of scary stories.

FEAR STREET ORIGIN STORY

I had written a bunch of standalone teen horror novels, such as *Blind Date*, *Twisted*, and *Beach House*.

But I knew that in order to create a successful series, I needed something more. I needed a location that was scary enough to draw readers in and a concept that was flexible enough to allow for a variety of characters and plotlines.

That's when it hit me: What if there was a small, normal town, but one street in that town was cursed? One street had a totally evil history, and anyone who moved to that street or walked on it had terrible things happen to them.

We came up with the name for the location and the series: Fear Street.

To flesh out the series, we created a whole backstory for the Fear family. They had cursed the street with their evil powers — going back to witchcraft and colonial times, and the terrible things that happened. We even created a rival family, the Goode family, who had been at odds with the Fears for generations. That was part of the legend, part of the legacy.

And so, we began writing the *Fear Street* books. Each one featured a new cast of characters, but all were connected by the sinister legacy of Fear Street.

CHAPTER TEN

PUBLICATION & BEYOND

56. DO SCHOOL VISITS.

Most children's book authors cultivate a fan base by doing school visits. You might start out locally to arrange speaking engagements and events. Getting attention for books is easier with kids because word of mouth is the primary way kids gain interest in things. They talk about books to each other in school, and it's wonderful.

57. SEARCH FOR BOOK FAIRS.

There are book fairs all around the country and at all times throughout the year. They're all over and it's great to appear, sign books, and go on panels. Many of these events look for authors to attend, so applying or reaching out to be there is a good idea. There are many local events, and there are also bigger ones such as the Miami Book Fair, the Tucson Festival of Books, and the Los Angeles Times

Festival of Books. These book festivals are invaluable and a great way to introduce yourself to other authors and to meet the crowds of readers.

58. KNOW WHO'S BUYING BOOKS.

Contact the people who actually buy books. Even if you're a children's book author, you'll be wanting to focus on talking to teachers, parents, and librarians. Kids don't buy their own books unless it's a school book fair or a school book club. Even then, the parents are involved. So it's very important to try to reach these gatekeepers as much as you can.

59. UTILIZE SOCIAL MEDIA FOR MARKETING.

Publishers will often expect you to do your own marketing, meaning that they expect you to use your social media accounts to promote and help sell your book.

I use social media a lot, and though I occasionally promote a book on them, that's not the main purpose. I do a lot of promotion, but I try to disguise it by doing other things so it doesn't look like I'm just selling all the time. I make sure to have some variety. I put a lot of funny stuff on Twitter, a lot of other news, and I talk to people. It's a fine balance.

I also love to do Q&A sessions. Those work very well.

People really like them. Q&A sessions are great ways to hear what's on readers' minds — what they're interested in and what they want to know about. They're all 20- and 30-somethings and they're the ones who grew up with *Goosebumps*. And it's so great to have a forum, to have a place where they all are, where I can hear from them and talk to them.

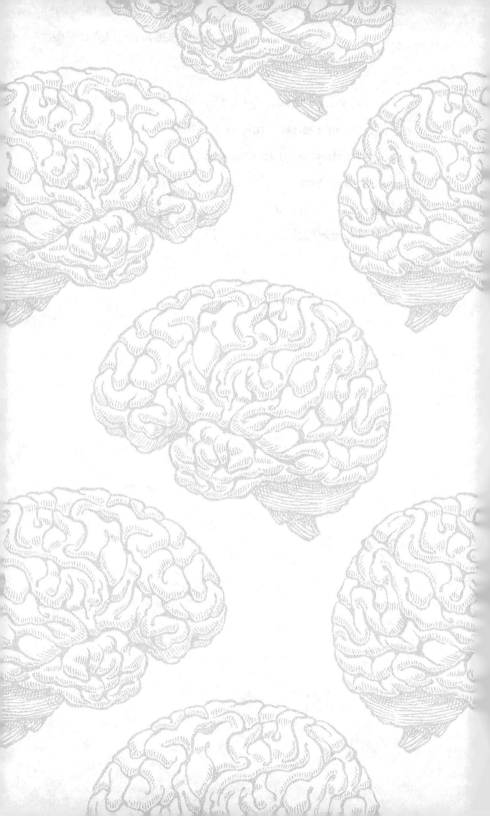

CHAPTER ELEVEN

LEARN FROM THE BEST

60. LEARN STORYCRAFT FROM RAY BRADBURY.

I'll never forget the first Bradbury story I read. It was unlike anything I had ever experienced. The words on the page were so beautifully crafted that they conjured up a vivid world in my mind. Bradbury's stories had it all — humor, suspense, twists, and horror.

Whenever kids ask me for scary book recommendations, I always suggest *Something Wicked This Way Comes*, one of Bradbury's most famous works. The book captured my imagination and inspired me to write my own stories.

Years later, I had the chance to meet Ray Bradbury himself at a book festival in Los Angeles. I was nervous to approach him, but my wife encouraged me to do so. When I finally mustered up the courage to speak to him, he was so kind and gracious that it brought me to tears. He told me that I was a hero to many people, and I'll never forget how much that meant to me.

61. LEARN PLOT FROM AGATHA CHRISTIE.

When it comes to suspenseful plots, there's no one quite like Agatha Christie. She had a masterful ability to create compelling plots, and I've often adapted Christie's plots for my own stories. While I don't always rely on murder as the central conflict, I've learned from Christie's ability to keep readers guessing and to use unexpected twists to keep the story fresh and engaging.

In the end, what I admire most about Agatha Christie is her ability to create stories that stay with readers long after they've turned the final page. Her mastery of plot is something that every writer can learn from, and her influence can be seen in countless books and movies to this day. For me, she remains the ultimate storyteller — one whose work continues to inspire and thrill readers around the world.

62. LEARN CREEPY FROM STEPHEN KING.

When it comes to writing horror, Stephen King's *Pet Sematary* is at the top of my list of favorite stories. What I love about *Pet Sematary* is how King takes a seemingly innocent idea — bringing a beloved pet back to life —

and turns it into something truly horrifying. The idea of resurrection is always tempting, but the consequences of bringing something back from the dead are often far worse than we can imagine.

When I finally met Stephen King at the Edgar Awards a few years ago, we had a friendly chat about our work. He jokingly accused me of using up every theme park plot idea. I took it as a compliment — there's no greater praise than being compared to a master of horror like him.

In the end, *Pet Sematary* remains one of the creepiest and most unforgettable books I've ever read. Its influence can be seen in countless horror stories and movies today, and its ability to terrify and captivate readers is a testament to King's masterful storytelling. For any aspiring horror writers out there, it's definitely worth a read — if you dare.

CHAPTER TWELVE
THAT'S A WRAP!

Well, I think we've come to the end. You know all my secrets now. I've told you everything I know — and everything I don't know!

I tried to break it all down into little pieces and short lessons — tips and tricks. And now that you've finished the book, I hope you'll sit down and **write something**.

Ready? I've added some resources to help guide you on your way.

And here's a bonus: I've included twenty story ideas you are welcome to use. Go ahead. Try one out!

As you write, remember to enjoy yourself. Remember that writing is **fun**.

Thanks for joining me here. And **stay scary**, everyone!

RL Stine

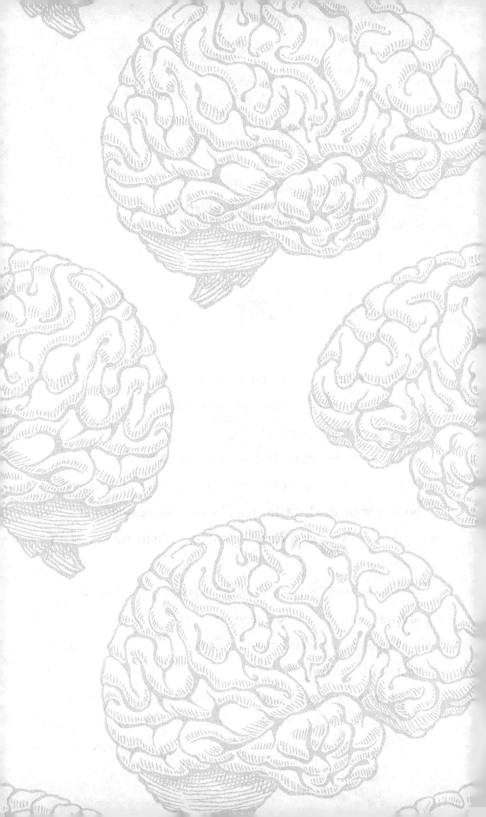

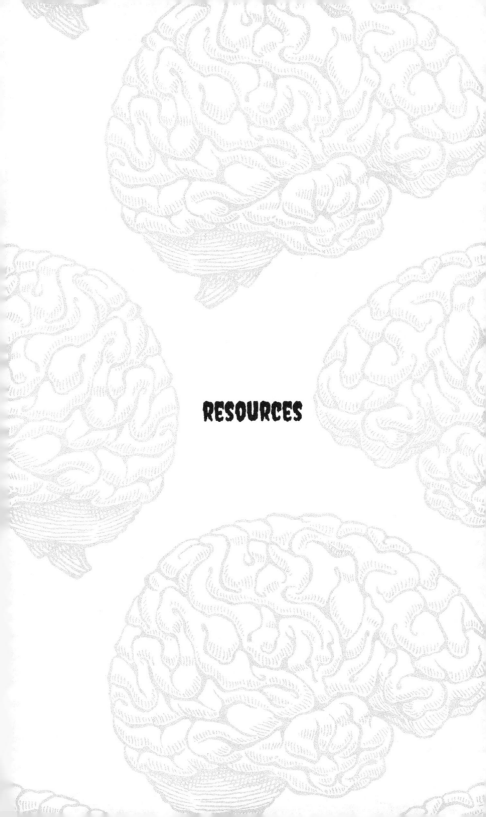

RESOURCES

TWENTY STORY IDEAS

Here's something a little extra for you: Twenty scary story ideas that you can use for kids.

I mentioned earlier that I can tell you how to go about finding ideas, but I can't really tell you how to get an idea. So here are twenty good, scary ideas that you're welcome to use for writing horror for kids. I've done a lot of these, but you can take them and make them your own. Feel free to take any one of them. Use them all or don't use any — whatever you want to do!

1. A creepy doll comes to life.
2. A scene from a nightmare comes true the next day.
3. Days go by, and your parents don't come home.
4. You feel yourself slowly becoming a monster.
5. Your friends start to disappear, and no one else notices.
6. You're lost in the woods, and you don't know how you

got there.

7. You're inhabited by a ghost that controls you and makes you do crazy things.

8. You have no reflection in the mirror.

9. The teacher is a monster, but no one will believe you.

10. You hypnotize your brother, and you can't snap him out of it.

11. A fortune teller reveals that you are evil.

12. Someone follows you home, and it's your exact double.

13. You find a diary that tells the future.

14. Every time you wake up, you're a different person.

15. Your parents explain that you are actually an alien from another planet.

16. You know someone is watching you day and night from the house across the street.

17. You realize you are shrinking.

18. While reading a scary book, you realize that you're a character in it.

19. Someone is living in your mirror.

20. Everyone knows the new neighbors are vampires, and the kids invite you over for a sleepover.

RELATED EXERCISES TO GET YOU GOING

People talk about getting writer's block all of the time. and one question I get most often is how to overcome it. Something that might make me unique is that I've never gotten writer's block before — not once! I would think that a way to get over it would be to start with smaller, more fun exercises that can get you going or wriggle you out of a rut.

So, I've provided different exercises to help you out. The following pages have an exercise listed at the top and space for you to write underneath.

That doesn't mean you can only practice these exercises once! Grab a notebook or journal, dust off that old typewriter, dedicate a document on your computer to your writing...it doesn't matter where you practice, it just matters that you do!

Write down three times you remember feeling truly scared.

_____

_____

_____

_____

_____

_____

_____

_____

_____

_____

_____

02

*Take a vivid memory that you have
and write it with a scary twist.*

03

Make a list of horror titles you'd be interested in reading
yourself. Make them funny, dramtic, weird - switch it up!

_____

_____

_____

_____

_____

_____

_____

_____

_____

_____

_____

_____

_____

Spend an hour in a place with lots of people, watch them, and write down any imaginative ideas that come to mind.

Try developing a horror plot, either from my previous list or an idea of your own. Try to come up with a few scenes, and if it feels like it's working, take it further.

06

*Write something in third-person, then write the same scene
from a first-person point of view.*

07

Identify an author you enjoy reading and write a scene mimicking that author's style. Try this again with another author who writes very differently.

_____

_____

_____

_____

_____

_____

_____

_____

_____

_____

_____

_____

_____

_____

Take a scene you've already written, then rewrite it using only dialogue.

_____

_____

_____

_____

_____

_____

_____

_____

_____

_____

_____

_____

_____

_____

_____

_____

09

Write a scene from one of my potential storiess and make it as scary as you can. Remember to do the following: Slow down the pace to build suspense. Don't skip over any detail.

_____

_____

_____

_____

_____

_____

_____

_____

_____

_____

_____

_____

_____

_____

_____

_____

Write a follow-up scene to the previous one and lighten the mood with a good balance of humor.

_____

_____

_____

_____

_____

_____

_____

_____

_____

_____

_____

_____

_____

Write a description that speaks to all five senses.

_____

_____

_____

_____

_____

_____

_____

_____

_____

_____

_____

_____

_____

_____

_____

_____

_____

Make character sheets (pg. xx). If you have no characters of your own, then make them for characters from your favorite book.

_____

_____

_____

_____

_____

_____

_____

_____

_____

_____

_____

_____

_____

_____

Take a place that you go often and write the scariest situation that could come from being there. Remember to be conscious of your reader - be scary to your audience , not just yourself!

_____

_____

_____

_____

_____

_____

_____

_____

_____

_____

_____

_____

_____

_____

_____

_____

14

Take an inanimate object and turn it into a scary monster.
Write a short description of your creature.

_____

_____

_____

_____

_____

_____

_____

_____

_____

_____

_____

_____

_____

_____

Write down a scary creature or situation. Take it further by increasing the horror factor of it. Take it further again, seeing how far you can go to make the initial thing as frightening ass can be.

_____

_____

_____

_____

_____

_____

_____

_____

_____

_____

_____

_____

_____

_____

Brainstorm things to include for a specific idea. Write down anything and everything that you could work into a story about this idea.

_____

_____

_____

_____

_____

_____

_____

_____

_____

_____

_____

_____

_____

_____

17

Practice giving feedback and opinions to know what you want from other people. Take any work (book, artwork, movie, etc.) and write down what you think about it. What do you like? What do you dislike? What stood out to you the most? How did this work make you feel?

_____

_____

_____

_____

_____

_____

_____

_____

_____

_____

_____

_____

_____

Write the ending of a scene without writing the beginning.

_____

_____

_____

_____

_____

_____

_____

_____

_____

_____

_____

_____

_____

_____

_____

Create a schedule. Block out times in your day where you can write. Stick to that schedule.

Schedule

5:00	
6:00	
7:00	
8:00	
9:00	
10:00	
11:00	
12:00	

13:00	
14:00	
15:00	
16:00	
17:00	
18:00	
19:00	
20:00	
21:00	
22:00	
23:00	
00:00	

20

Write something that you've always wanted to write. Have fun with it, and don't stress about making it perfect. Remember, first drafts are never the final product. Just write this thing, and celebrate that you've actually done it!

_____

_____

_____

_____

_____

_____

_____

_____

_____

_____

_____

_____

_____

_____

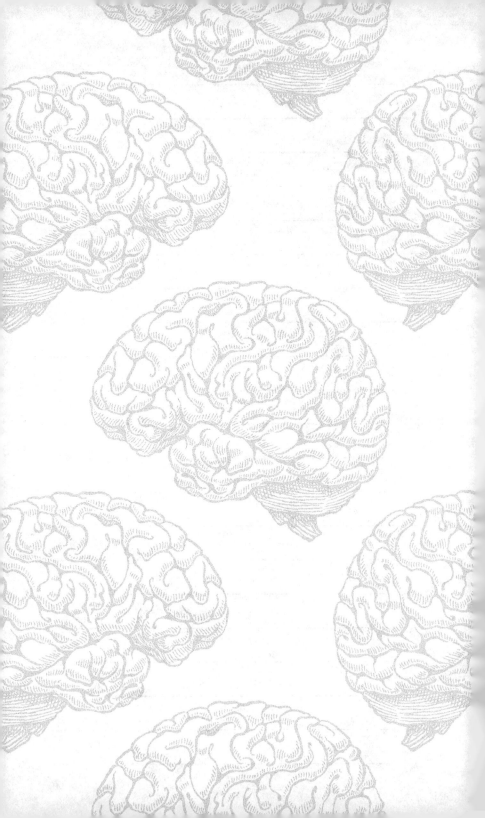

HOW DOES THIS REALLY WORK?

Now that you've loosened your pen and have gotten your writing going, let's dive into fleshing out your story.

I have given you the tips and tricks to follow, but here are some personal examples of those things in play — some of my books in their unfinished stages.

I am going to take you through the phases of writing, starting with the premise of one of my stories, a side-by-side comparison of an original story outline, as well as the revised outline, and ending with editorial notes that I had to implement after my first draft. These will all be from different titles of mine so you can get standalone examples for each stage.

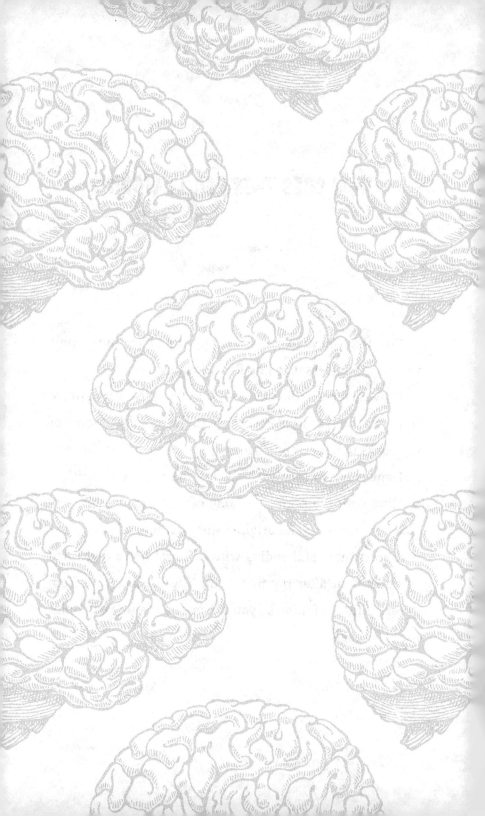

SLAPPY IN DREAMLAND

WHERE IT ALL BEGINS: THE PREMISE

Once you've gotten your ideal formulated and the details cooking, you have to be able to tell a condensed version of your story. You have to know where you'll be going before you start — otherwise you'll just be wandering around in your writing.

The example I'm providing is the premise for Slappy in Dreamland. Through it, you will see the setup of the book. The details aren't included, but key pieces of information and dialogue are laid out.

Doing this serves as a roadmap — you could say that it's the skeleton of the outline before you go in and flesh out the details, twists, and conflicts. It's another effective trick to use in order to get your story moving while at its beginning stages.

Goosebumps
SlappyWorld

SLAPPY IN DREAMLAND

R.L. STINE

SCHOLASTIC

Image courtesy of Scholastic

SLAPPY IN DREAMLAND: PREMISE

Narrated by Richard Hsieh (*auction winner*), 12. Richard is working on a thousand-piece jigsaw puzzle and has only ten or twelve pieces to go. As he works, he talks to his ventriloquist dummy, Slappy, his favorite birthday gift and his constant companion. His mom interrupts. She is a doctor who runs a sleep lab, and it's Bring-Your-Kid-to-Work day. Richard asks if he can bring Slappy, and she relents.

At the lab, she explains how she treats people who are having trouble sleeping. They go to bed in separate lab rooms and she hooks them up with many electrodes. Then she follows their sleep patterns on monitors.

Richard insists that she demonstrate on Slappy. Dr. Hsieh thinks it's a funny idea. She connects Slappy to a monitor that isn't being used. She starts to show Richard the results on the screen—but she stops and gasps. "This doesn't make any sense!" she exclaims. "I'm seeing brain activity. But that's impossible! That can't happen with a lifeless dummy."

She unhooks Slappy and hands him back to Richard. "There must be a problem with my electrode system."

That night, Richard puts Slappy at the foot of his bed, which he does every night. In his sleep, Richard has a frightening dream. Slappy pulls the covers off Richard in the dream, and wakes him. Slappy talks! He demands that Richard become his servant for life. When Richard refuses, Slappy bites his arm and won't let go. The dummy laughs as Richard howls in pain.

Richard wakes up. Slappy is in his place. The bed covers are still on. "What a horrible nightmare. And it was so real!" But wait. Why is Richard's arm red and sore? Was it just from sleeping on it?

The next day, Richard's cousin Willow arrives to stay for a few days while her parents are away. Willow is in his class at school. They are both very excited about the annual class sleepover at the town zoo. Organized by the zoo, there is a big dinner and a show of the animals, and they all sleep in sleeping bags in the giraffe house. Richard and Willow are painting a big mural with many zoo animals on it to show off at the overnight.

He tells Willow about his nightmare. She laughs: "You should put that dummy in the closet at night." She teases him about the jigsaw puzzle: "What do you do with it when it's finished? Mess it up and start again?"

That night, Richard has another terrifying dream. He is on the school bus. The bus goes faster... faster... out of control. Several hair-raising near-misses. Richard screams for the driver to slow down. The driver slowly turns around. It's Slappy! Slappy laughs. The bus crashes. Everything falls apart, tears into a thousand pieces.

Richard wakes up very shaken. Slappy is still in his place at the bottom of the bed. Richard gets up—and stares at his jigsaw puzzle. It's been pulled apart, completely undone. How can that be?

Willow bursts into breakfast, very upset. She had a nightmare about Slappy, too. In her dream, she and Richard were painting their mural. Slappy appeared and demanded they both be his servants. When they refused, Slappy started splashing thick waves of paint over them. Willow woke up choking.

Richard doesn't understand. How could they both dream about Slappy? Reluctantly, he puts Slappy in a closet. They go to work on their mural—and it has been ruined. The animals have been painted over, and a big face of a grinning Slappy covers the painting.

The next night, they both have another frightening dream about Slappy. The next morning, they examine the dummy and find the secret words on a slip of paper in his pocket. Willow: "It says the words bring Slappy to life. Did you ever read them aloud?" Richard: "Only once. When I first got him."

They decide the nightmares won't stop until they get rid of Slappy. They take him on a town bus, ride to the end of the line, and dump Slappy in the woods.

That night, Slappy appears to both of them in terrifying nightmares. "You'll be sorry," Slappy tells them in their dreams. "You'll be sorry you sent me away. I'll haunt your dreams forever!"

The next morning, Slappy is back on the front porch. What can they do? Now they are afraid to go to sleep. They put Slappy back in the closet and stay up all night. What are those noises? Is he moving around in the closet? Is that him laughing?

The next day, they are exhausted as the class goes to the zoo for the class sleepover. They try to have fun, but they are very sleepy and tense. After the dinner and the animal demonstration, everyone goes to sleep in sleeping bags. And tonight—*Slappy invades ALL their dreams.*

Slappy makes the whole class get up and sleepwalk to the Jungle Preserve. The kids wake up, stunned, as they are being stalked by the zoo's Bengal tigers. A frantic rescue by the zookeepers. No one knows how this could happened. Except for Richard and Willow.

Richard believes that something happened when Slappy was hooked up in the sleep lab. It gave him the power to appear in dreams. He has an idea to get Slappy out of his dreams. He asks his mom to take him to her sleep lab and hook him up to the same machine that she used for Slappy. His thought: The only way to stop this and defeat Slappy is for him to invade Slappy's dreams.

Mom hooks him up. Richard forces himself to go to sleep. Will this work?

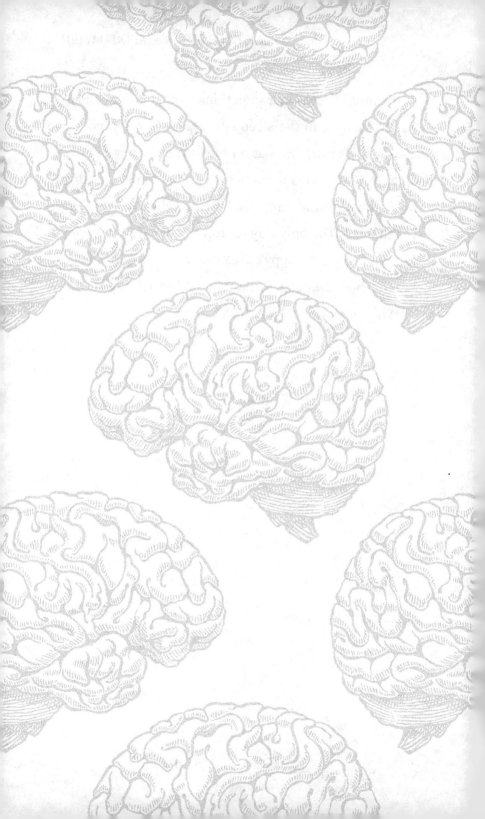

I AM SLAPPY'S EVIL TWIN

WRITING AN OUTLINE: BEFORE & AFTER

On the pages that follow are two versions of my outline for *I Am Slappy's Evil Twin*. On the left-hand page, you'll find an example of my original outline. On the right-hand page, you'll see the final version, how my outline was ultimately changed after revisions.

As you look at the two side-by-side, pay attention to how quickly the revised version moves, while in the rough draft, the real action doesn't begin until Chapter 15.

I AM SLAPPY'S EVIL TWIN: FIRST DRAFT

1.   1920. A farm village. Puppeteer Franz Mahar working in his workshop, finishing a ventriloquist dummy: "You are made of the finest coffin wood, and I have given you the dark powers I learned on my tour of Europe. Someone will pay a million dollars for you when they learn of the abilities and powers I have given you." But wait—a pounding on the door. Who is beating on the door like that? Mahar opens the door to find the entire village storming his cabin. They carry guns and torches. What do they want?

2.   They angrily accuse him of bringing bad luck to the village. The crops have withered and died, and the cows are all giving sour milk. "It's the doll!" they cry. "Look at that evil face. The doll has brought evil and bad fortune to our village." They grab the dummy. Mahar pleads with them: "No—it's my life's work. I beg you!" But the villagers build a tall bonfire, and they burn the dummy. As the flames consume it, the dummy blinks its eyes open and opens its mouth in a deafening scream.

3.   After watching the dummy burn, Mahar slinks back to his workshop. "The fools. The stupid fools," he mutters

I AM SLAPPY'S EVIL TWIN: FINAL REVISION

1. 1920. A farm village. Puppeteer Franz Mahar working in his workshop, finishing a ventriloquist dummy: "You are made of the finest coffin wood, and I have given you the dark powers I learned on my tour of Europe. Someone will pay a million dollars for you when they learn of the abilities and powers I have given you." But wait—a pounding on the door. Who is beating on the door like that? Mahar opens the door to find the entire village storming his cabin. They carry guns and torches. What do they want?

2. They angrily accuse him of bringing bad luck to the village. The crops have withered and died, and the cows are all giving sour milk. "It's the doll!" they cry. "Look at that evil face. The doll has brought evil and bad fortune to our village." They grab the dummy. Mahar pleads with them: "No—it's my life's work. I beg you!" But the villagers build a tall bonfire, and they burn the dummy. As the flames consume it, a scream of pain and horror rings out over the village.

3. The scream came from Mahar as he watched his dummy burn. The villagers warn him to stop his evil work.

bitterly. "Did they really think Id' give up my precious dummy so easily?" They burned one of Mahar's copies, a fake. He has two dummies on the shelf. He picks one up. "They burned a fake," he tells it. He and the two dummies toss back their heads and laugh.

* * *

4.   This year. A rambling old house on the edge of the woods. We meet Gabe Miller and his younger sister Gwinny (short for Gwyneth). "Did you know this house is haunted?" Gabe tells Gwinny. He likes to scare her because she's easily scared. He tells her a story about a boy who was murdered in the basement. "You can still hear him walking around at night. Once a week on Friday nights, he comes upstairs to haunt the people in this house. What night is it, Gwinny?" "Friday?" Gabe points: "Sssh. Listen. Do you hear something? There he is now!" Gwinny screams.

5.   It isn't a ghost. It's Grandpa Noah: "Are you scaring Gwinny again? Don't you ever get tired of scary ghost stories?" Gwinny: "I wasn't really scared. I just screamed because he expected me to." They are in Grandpa Noah's house. The grandparents are moving to Florida. This is a sad farewell. Touching goodbyes. "Take good care of my

"My work is over," he tells them, appearing to be a broken man. "You have destroyed my life's work." Mahar slinks back to his workshop. "The fools. The stupid fools," he mutters bitterly. "Did they really think Id' give up my precious dummy so easily?" They burned one of Mahar's copies, a fake. He has two dummies on the shelf. He picks one up. "They burned a fake, a useless lifeless hunk of wood," he tells it. He and the two dummies toss back their heads and laugh.

* * *

THIS YEAR

4. Narrated by Luke Harrison, 12. Luke, his sister Kelly, and their friend Jamal are in Luke's garage. They are building their own propane- powered drone for a school contest. Working very hard. It's complicated, but Jamal is a mechanical kid. He calls to Luke: Hey, what are you doing with the propane tank? Your dad said to stay away from it." Luke: "Just moving it out of the way. WHOOOPS!" The big tank slips out of his hands. Luke: "Look out! It's going to blow!" Kelly and Jamal scream.

5. Luke catches it and laughs. He was joking. He's always trying to scare people. "Guess I take after my dad."

aquarium," says Grandpa Noah. "There are some rare and valuable tropical fish in there."

Gwinny promises she'll feed them every day and clean the tank. Dad leaves to drive his parents to the airport. The Millers are staying for a week to help clean out the old house. Gabe: "Let's see what's in the basement." Gwinny is reluctant. Mom: "Promise you won't frighten Gwinny." Gabe: "I promise." He has his fingers crossed behind his back. "Follow me," he tells her.

6.   They step into the basement stairwell. He clicks the light. It doesn't go on. "Bulb must be out. Don't worry. There are more lights downstairs." He uses the flashlight on his phone. When he gets to the bottom of the stairs, Gabe starts to struggle. "Oh, wow. I've walked into something. Spider webs! So thick. They're wrapping me up. Help! The spiders—they're biting me! Help! They're biting!" Gwinny: "Stop joking, Gabe. You promised." He drops to his back, thrashing his arms, screaming. To her horror, Gwinny realizes he isn't joking!

7.   She finds a broom. Frantically sweeps the spiders and thick webbing off him. Finally, he stands up: "Didn't Grandpa ever clean this place?" He clicks on a dim ceiling bulb. Both of them cry out. The basement is filled with

Luke's dad is owner of Horror House Films. He produces horror movies. Kelly and Jamal are angry. "Dad said not to go near the propane tank unless he's here with us. We don't want to BE in a horror movie. A strange shrill voice says: "Well, you're in one now!" The startled kids turn—and see two identical ventriloquist dummies standing at the garage door.

6.   Dummy: "You're in a world of horror. Welcome to our world!" Luke: "Who's there? Who is making them talk?" Dummy: "Who's pulling your strings? We'll be asking the questions from now on!" Mr. Harrison calls from the driveway. "Hey, are you kids in the garage?" The two dummies collapse in a heap to the ground. Dad: "Hey, whyd' you take these dummies from my car?" Luke: "We didn't." Dad: "Oh, I suppose they got up and walked on their own?!" Jamal: "Please tell us you're joking. Those dummies talked to us." Harrison laughs: "You must have read the script to my new movie, I Married A Dummy." He picks up the dummies and turns to leave. "Kelly: Please believe us, Dad. The dummies walked and talked." Dad: "Don't kid a kidder. Help me carry one of them up to the attic, Luke." Luke takes one and slings it over his shoulder. He feels wooden fingers squeeze around his hand. They tighten. Tighten. "Dad— help! It's hurting me!"

ghosts! No. Wait. It's furniture covered in sheets. Gwinny: "It's too creepy down here. Let's go back upstairs." Gabe: "But Grandpa Noah collected all kinds of cool stuff. And he said we could have whatever we want." He starts to explore. Cries out when something brushes the back of his neck. It's just the sleeve of an old shirt hanging from a line. They find a lot of cool things, strange objects, photos. They suddenly stop when they hear scraping footsteps. "We're not alone down here!" They freeze. And hear a whisper: "Gabe... I'm going to haunt you." Gabe cries out: "Huh? Did you hear that, too?" "Gabe... I'm going to haunt you... FOREVER!"

8.   "It... it's the ghost of the basement!" Gabe chokes out. Then they hear laughter. Mom steps out of the shadows: "You're always scaring Gwinny, Gabe. I wanted to show you what it's like." Gabe grumbles: "Not cool, Mom." Mom asks them to come upstairs and help her pack some books into boxes. Gabe begs for ten more minutes. Mom goes back upstairs. They explore. Gwinny: "Hey, what's that?" Something looks like a mummy, all wrapped up. Gabe slowly unwraps it. A head appears—a pale face, eyes shut. It's a dead body!

9.   Gabe drops it and the head clonks on the floor. It's some kind of doll. They unwrap it. It's a ventriloquist

7.   Dad spins around. The dummy's arm is hanging limply. "You can carry a joke too far, Luke. The three kids follow him to his horror collection in the attic: The mummy's hand from the original Mummy film. Frankenstein's huge shoes from the original film. A shark jaw from Jaws. It's like a horror museum. Jamal is freaked. He doesn't like scary movies, and this collection gives him the creeps. "Nothing to be scared about," Kelly tells him. "It's just a bunch of costumes and props." Jamal has trouble breathing. He takes out an inhaler. "It's like he has this strange ability to sense danger," Luke explains to Dad. "But why is he wheezing now?" Dad asks. "There's no danger here." They carry the dummies to a large glass display case. Dad: "These dummies are valuable antiques. We need to keep them safe and sound until I need them for the movie. Then I'm going to sell them for a ton of money." He locks them in the glass case and puts they key on a nearby table. "Don't touch them, kids." His phone rings. He has to take the call. Disappears downstairs. The kids stare at the dummies on their backs in the case. They are identical, except one has olive green eyes, the other black eyes. The kids gasp as the dummy with green eyes suddenly raises a wooden hand and begins tapping on the glass.

8.   Tap tap tap. A terrifying sound. Both dummies are

dummy. They want to show it to Mom. Gabe starts to lift it up, and the wooden hand swings up and smacks him hard in the face. "Ow!" He accuses Gwinny. She says she didn't touch it.

They take it to Mom: "Grandpa Noah used to entertain at kids' parties. I'm pretty sure his grandfather made the dummy." Gabe: "Can I keep it?"

Gwinny: "No. It's mine. I saw it first." They fight over it. Gabe insists he wants to do an act with it for his scary YouTube channel. Mom says Gabe can have it. She'll buy something nice for Gwinny. Gwinny is only a little appeased. As Gabe goes to pick up the dummy, it slaps him in the face again. "Stop it, Gwinny!" Gabe snaps. She swears she didn't touch it. Gabe stares at the dummy's grinning face. He feels a little shiver as it appears to stare back at him.

10. The next day. Gabe practicing with the dummy in the room he's staying in upstairs. He named it Mickey. He performs for Gwinny. She says he's a terrible ventriloquist—and his jokes are lame. "Cousin Harvey is coming to stay with us. His parents have to go away and they're dropping him off here. Maybe he'll like your dumb jokes." Gabe: "Harvey is such a wimp. He'll probably be terrified of the dummy. He's terrified of everything." Gwinny: "Mom says we have to promise not to scare him this time. Last time,

tapping on the lid. Kelly: "They want us to let them out."
Jamal: "No way!" Luke: Maybe we should do it." He pulls out
his phone. "We let them out of the case, and I'll video the
whole thing. It'll prove to Dad that we weren't lying, that
the dummies can walk and talk." Jamal begs them not to.
He's terrified. Tap tap tap tap. What should they do? Luke
reaches for the key...

9.   Kelly takes her phone and gets ready to make a
video. Luke turns the key in the lock and raises the lid. All
three kids gasp as the dummies sit up. "Thanks for the fresh
air!" Jamal: "Huh? Dummies can't talk!" Dummy:
"Who you calling dummy, dummy?" the dummies
scramble out of the case. Jamal backs away. Kelly is getting
the whole thing on video. The green-eyed dummy laughs:
"Don't be so scared. We're only terrifying! Hahaha. My name
is Slappy. And my twin's name is Snappy. You can call us
Master!" Snappy: "Don't be so harsh, Slappy. You're scaring
them." Slappy laughs again: "You're going to love doing
everything we order you to do." Kelly: "I've got enough on
video to show Dad. Let's go." But Slappy leaps forward and
grabs her phone and heaves it across the attic. It smashes
into a glass statuette, which shatters. Before the kids can
move, they hear Dad running up the stairs: "What's going
on? Did I hear broken glass?"

you jumped out of the closet and grabbed him in the middle of the night, and he shook for two days." Gabe laughs. Gwinny leaves his room. He gets a Skype call from Grandpa Noah. They talk about Florida for a while. Gabe (holds up dummy): "Look what I found in your basement." To Gabe's surprise, Grandpa cries: "Oh no! NO! You weren't supposed to find that." Gabe: "Grandpa—why?" Grandpa: "Get rid of it. Get rid of it!"

11.   Gabe tries to get his grandpa to explain. But the skype call is cut off. Why was Grandpa so upset? Gabe is curious now. He gazes at the dummy. Did its grin just get wider? He sets up his phone on a tripod and does an episode of his YouTube series. He does a short routine with Mickey the dummy. But Gwinny interrupts his show. She says she found the dummy and it should be hers. They fight. He's angry she ruined his video. He chases her out. Puts his phone away. He's thinking about Grandpa's reaction. Decides to look up the dummy in the Wikipedia. He stares at the page. "Oh, wow. I don't believe it!"

12.   He's dying to show Gwinny the Wikipedia page, but his parents call them downstairs. Harvey is coming to stay for a week, and the parents order them to be nice to him. "It's his birthday. No one wants to be terrified on

10. Dad sees the broken statuette and is very alarmed. "The dummies did it!" Luke cries. They turn—and see that both dummies are back in the case, flat on their backs. The statuette was very rare and valuable. Kelly: "I can prove the dummies did it." She picks up her phone. It's wrecked. It won't work. Dad is furious. "You've got to stop this dumb joke about the dummies. You're both grounded for lying about the statuette. Jamal tries to defend them, but it's no use. Mr. Harrison ushers them downstairs. As Luke starts down the stairs, Slappy winks at him and waves bye-bye.

11. Later, Luke goes to bed. He's awakened by a sound at his bedroom door. He looks up and sees the dummy standing there. What's behind it? Another dummy. They invade his room, followed by two more dummies. Four dummies, walking stiffly, moving steadily toward his bed. The dummies whisper in frightening raspy tones: "I'm Slappy... I'm Snappy... I'm Slappy... I'm Snappy...

12. Luke wakes up, badly shaken. It had to be a nightmare—right? He sits up in bed. He hears footsteps out in the hall. The dummies. He listens to them, coming closer... closer. Luke bursts out of his room, into the dark hall. He sees a figure lurking nearby. He lets out a hoarse cry—and tackles it.

his birthday." Gabe: "It's too easy to scare him. He jumps if you touch him. He's a bigger scaredy-cat than Gwinny." That starts an argument between the two kids. Gabe: "Stop. I have to tell you what I just read about the dummy." Dad: "No. No dummy. Put it away. I mean it. It will only scare Harvey." Gabe protests: "You won't believe what I read. The dummy can come to life." Gwinny gasps. Dad: "Stop it right now, Gabe. No scary stories. Save them for your YouTube show." Gabe grumbles to himself.

Then he pulls Gwinny upstairs to his room. He shows her his laptop screen. "Look. Look what it says about this dummy."

13.   Gwinny reads the Wiki page in disbelief: "His name is Slappy? And he can come to life? And he's horribly evil?" Gabe: "Yes. You just say the secret words, and he's supposed to come to life. That's why Grandpa Noah didn't want me to have it." Gwinny backs away, suddenly frightened: "You're not going to do it—are you?" A grin spreads over Gabe's face. Gwinny pleads with him not to try it. "Don't worry. The secret words aren't on the Wiki Page," he tells her. "Maybe they're hidden on the dummy or something. I don't know." Gwinny breathes a sigh of relief. They hear the doorbell ring downstairs. Harvey has arrived. Mom shouts: "Come downstairs and greet your cousin." Gabe puts the dummy

13. It's Kelly. She thought she heard noises upstairs in the attic. They listen. It's silent now. Kelly: "We have to prove to Dad that we're not liars. He has to know the truth—those two dummies are alive!" Luke grabs the little GoPro video camera his dad gave him for his birthday. They gather their courage and climb up to the attic. Very creepy with all the horror movie memorabilia. They turn on the attic light. Luke raises the camera. They step up to the glass case. It's empty. Before they can move, a wooden hand grips Luke's shoulder from behind. Both kids scream.

14. "Enough playtime, kiddies. Let's make a REAL horror film!" Slappy screams. Snappy: "Slappy, play nice. Why can't you ever get along with others?" Slappy tells his twin to shut his wooden mouth. He grabs up the camera and turns it on the kids. "That's it—scream! Let's hear you scream!" He slams the camera into Luke's hands. "Okay, get a good close- up of ME now. Get a good profile shot. Know what I'm calling this movie? It's called The Boy in the Glass Coffin." He hands the camera to Kelly. He grabs Luke again and with incredible strength, lifts him off the floor.

Luke thrashes and struggles. Snappy: "Be gentle, Slappy. You don't want to hurt anybody—do you?" Slappy ignores Snappy and carries Luke to the glass case and drops him into it. "Keep filming! This is awesome!

down. "Maybe I'll bring him to life later. Just to give Harvey a scare." As Gwinny runs downstairs, Gabe glances back at the dummy. Did it just wink at him? No. That's impossible.

14. Gwinny greets Harvey. We can see that he's a tense kid. They all chat for a bit. Dad: "Where's Gabe?" Gwinny: "Upstairs, I guess." Gabe appears a few minutes later. He teases Harvey about the last visit, how they scared him. "I won't do that again," Gabe promises, with a devilish smile on his face. Harvey: "I'm trying to be braver now that I'm turning twelve." The doorbell rings. Harvey: "It might be my parents. Maybe I forgot and left something in the car." He pulls open the front door—and lets out a startled shriek. The dummy is standing on the front stoop, grinning at him.

15. "He's ALIVE!" Gabe screams. Harvey screams again, staggers back, stumbles, and falls to the floor. Gwinny is horrified. Gabe laughs: "I stood him up there. Just a little joke." Dad: "How did he ring the doorbell?"

Gabe raises his phone: "The doorbell ring came from my phone." Parents are angry: "I warned you to put that dummy away. Put it in a closet. I don't want to see it again." Harvey insists he's not afraid of it; he was only startled. He goes to pick up the dummy, and it slaps him in the face.

Parents take Harvey to a spare bedroom to get him

What a scene!" Inside the glass case, Luke screams: "Let me out! What are you doing?" Slappy locks the case—and tosses the key across the attic.

Luke pounds on the glass. Kelly screams but she is afraid to stop filming.

Slappy: "Perfect! Let's see some real terror! Bang on the glass. Scream, Kelly! I smell an Academy Award for this! Keep pounding, Luke! Good! Now you're red in the face, Luke! Excellent! Love that panic! Keep screaming. Keep it up, everybody!"

15. Snappy: "You're playing too rough, Slappy. Why do you always want to hurt people?" Slappy: "Shut up, Snappy. You know, your head would look good in a wood chipper." Snappy: "That hurts my feelings. Apologize." Slappy: "Apologize because you're a whining wimp? Just shut your wooden trap!" Kelly leaps into action: "You can't do that to my brother!"

Slappy: "I can do whatever I want. Did you forget? I'm Slappy!" With a roar, Kelly leaps on him, tackles him to the floor. They struggle. Kelly frees herself. She runs downstairs shouting for her dad. Dad, half-asleep, comes running. She pulls him up to the attic. He sees Luke locked inside the glass case. Kelly: "Now do you believe us?"

settled in. Gwinny and Gabe take the dummy to Gabe's room. Gwinny: "Give him to me, Gabe. You'll only get in trouble if you keep him. He should be mine, anyway." They fight over the dummy. Have a tug-of-war with it. And a slip of paper falls out of the dummy's jacket. The secret words! Gabe grabs it out of Gwinny's hand. She begs him not to read them. But he raises the paper to his face and reads the words out loud: BAHKU RAMA DUBBA MOONDEE ARAMMUS.

16. They stare at the dummy. Did its eyes blink open? Or were they already open? Gabe stretches him out on his back on the bed. "Get up, Slappy. Let's see you sit up." The dummy doesn't move. He sits Slappy up. "Can you walk? Can you say something?" It remains lifeless. Gwinny laughs: "It's a total fake. And you fell for it!" She leaves. Gabe is very disappointed. He props the dummy in a corner. He goes to sleep. He dreams that Slappy comes to life and walks all over the house. He wakes up shaking—and sees that the dummy is gone!

16. Dad looks on floor. The dummies are lifeless, tangled in a heap. Dad: "Did you really think you could fool me with this trick? Where's the key? Let your brother out." Kelly finds the key. They let Luke out. Dad is really angry: "Don't ever try to trick me like that again." But, wait—the GoPro camera. Luke grabs it, turns the screen to Dad. Oh no. In the excitement, he forgot to push record. Dad: "I'm taking the dummies to the studio tomorrow to begin filming our movie. So you can stop worrying about them. And no more dumb stunts." Back in his room, Luke is frustrated and angry that Dad won't believe them. He looks out his bedroom window—and sees the two dummies in the back yard, doing a crazy dance in the moonlight. He gasps and pulls the blind shut. Should I tell Dad? Oh, what's the use?

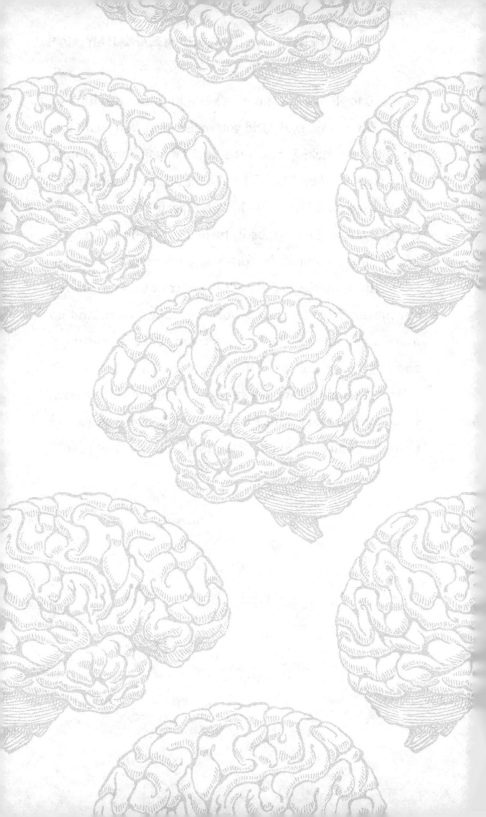

SLIME DOESN'T PAY!

LEANING IN &LEARNING FROM FEEDBACK

From the outline, you were able to whip up your first draft of your manuscript and send it over to someone to read and give notes. Finding someone to do this might be challenging, but once you do, you need to make sure to ask the questions we talked about before.

When they're going through what you've written, asked them to write some notes on what they think of it. Hopefully when they're done, you'll have nothing but praise for being a genius storyteller!

More likely, you'll get a compliment here and there, and several pages of things to change.

I've included the shorted editorial notes I received from my first draft of *Slime Doesn't Pay!* You'll see that in it, my editor pointed out the key points to focus on during my next round of revisions — both elements to change throughout the story, as well as details to include, alter, etc.

From here, we repeat this process until the book is solid.

BESTSELLING AUTHOR OF GOOSEBUMPS

R. L. STINE

SLIME DOESN'T PAY!

Image courtesy of Blackstone Publishing

SLIME DOESN'T PAY!
EDITORIAL NOTES

February 2, 2023

Hiya Bobby,

There are lots of fun laugh-out-loud lines in this manuscript, and I love Marta and Sophie.

I started to tell you some of the problems. Here they are in more detail:

The first issue is the lack of tension. Nothing happens in the first ninety pages to propel the reader to want to read on. The story lacks momentum and suspense and is basically a collection of bad boy incidents. They don't translate to any actual peril for our main character. They simply illustrate that Amy has an annoying brother, and believe me, after the first few examples, we get the point. Each behavior event is basically on the same level of badness as the others. Nothing escalates, and by the time we reach page 90, nothing more has happened beyond Arnie misbehaving.

A closer look at the incidents: At the sleepover, the pizza in the face incident works. This is a personal attack and we can start to empathize with Amy. But the burglar event doesn't work at all. An eight-year-old would never be mistaken for a grown man, so that incident will have to be rethought, and if we can make it more personal, it will feel less generic. For his misbehavior to have any weight on this night, and not merely be just bad boy behavior, there has to be a repercussion to his actions. So, by the end of the night, we have to hear that no one ever wants to come to a sleepover at Amy's again. (More about this later). Again, it has to be personal.

The script scattering (love that it's Fiddler!) feels random. He couldn't have known the wind would pick up that way and cause the pages to fly out the window. And there weren't any major repercussion from losing the pages. Nothing in Amy's life changed in any meaningful way from that particular act. She didn't respond to it in any way. It didn't move the story in any direction.

Next, Arnie splashes mud on her coat. No big deal. Yes, it was a new coat and a favorite, but it still comes off as just another nuisance. Nothing beyond that.

Arnie shoplifts, but this doesn't effect Amy at all. Just more bad behavior. Plus, after he gets caught, he's quickly let off the hook, so nothing has happened that actually increases the tension.

The bugs in the cake is a good event—it's personal. But it's too little too late.

Basically we have 90 pages of Amy complaining about Arnie him. For 90 pages she doesn't do anything. It's just a litany of Arnie's bad conduct. We have to wait till page

92 before she actually takes action. Ninety pages of bad behavior and whining isn't compelling. It's not a story a reader can become invested in.

In between these events, Amy does get attacked by the animal, but again, there is nothing in that scene that is actually frightening or changes anything. The beast comes after her but the action is totally diffused when it stops to lick a squirrel. Then she gets hit by a car, but not really, and she is fine. Then she's chased again by the animal, but he kinda disappears and nothing happens. (There are more notes about all this on the manuscript.) So we basically have a prolonged encounter that is static—the action, as it were, doesn't change anything. Amy doesn't do anything in response to it. The attack has absolutely no repercussions. It changes nothing in the story. It doesn't advance the plot in any way.

Again, nothing of any consequence happens to our main character for more than half the book. It's not much of a story at all and the reader loses interest fairly early on.

Since we don't want to think about a major plot revision, I have an idea about how you can add tension/suspense right from the start.

Begin the book with Amy addressing the reader: I did something horrible to my brother. I'm not kidding. I can't believe I did it. You're going to find out now what I did, but first I have to explain to you why I did it. Once you hear my side of the story, you won't hate me. You'll agree with me; I had no choice. My brother has always been a pain. But he was getting worse. He was becoming impossible. And then he did something unspeakable to me. And that's why I did what I did. Yes, what I did was hideous. But maybe you'll say you would have done the same thing. I really think you will. It all started at my sleepover...

In this way, we frontload the suspense. Have the reader wondering, what did he do to her that was so bad? And what did she do to him?

Then we go through the events, but each has to build in intensity and each has to be directly aimed at her. In between some of the events, have her break through and address the reader. Something like: I bet you're starting to see what I was going through. Are you saying, ok, he's annoying, but he's not that bad? Your brother/sister is worse. Well, just wait. There's no way your brother/sister is worse. I might have done something unforgivable to Arnie, but what he did to me was disgusting. Etc. Keep building the momentum with these interstitials.

This is how it might play out. (I've reordered some of the events): We start with the sleepover. It's something she's been looking forward to; she loves having her friends over— and Arnie ruins it. First, he pushes the pizza in her face.

Then he scares everyone by pretending the animal is still in the house. Then he XXXX. (This is where the burglar scene has to be tweaked.) The rest of the sleepover is okay, but Sophie and Marta make it clear that they're never coming to another sleepover at Amy's again.

We need a few more incidents here that escalate, each one making Amy's life more and more miserable. (You don't need as many as you have now—see page 7 of this letter for a note on filling out pages and manuscript length.)

After the incident(s) to come mentioned above, let's have him put the bugs in the cake.

Amy addresses the reader—you might think this is where I snapped. But it isn't. It gets much, much worse.

Then they go to the video store. But here, instead of Arnie putting the game in his pocket, he puts it in Amy's bag. SHE is accused of shoplifting. She's going to jail!

Amy addresses reader: Okay, you think this is it? This is where you'd probably do something hideous to your brother or sister if they almost got you sent to prison. Well, this wasn't it. But it was close to it. I might have calmed down from this. And not done the horrible thing to Arnie. Except for the next thing he did. That was the final straw. That's what made me snap...

Then she wakes up with the rude word on her forehead. No Photo day. She can't go to school for a week, etc.

Amy addresses reader: It was time for revenge.

Some other notes:

Why did Mom and Dad adopt Arnie if they knew he was a monster? Let's add in the beginning that Mom has a soft spot for animals. She can't even step on an ant. Amy explains: When a bee stings you, the stinger is left in your skin. When a bee stung Mom, she apologized to the bee for keeping it and tried to give it back. So...when Amy says there's an animal in the house from the woods and it attacked her, Mom says don't hurt it! And later on, when Mom reveals that they knew Arnie was a monster, she can say she felt bad for him; nobody wanted him, etc. It will mesh with her persona and feel totally natural.

Amy and the Monster: Amy immediately assumes that the creature is a monster. (She uses 'monster' and 'beast' interchangeably from the start.) We need to calibrate her reaction to it. Since most people believe monsters are imaginary creatures, she shouldn't naturally assume that this is one. In the house, when she first confronts it, they should all assume that it was some sort of animal from the woods. When she meets it again coming home from Sophie's house, she still thinks it's some kind of animal, but when it leaps on her, she realizes she's never seen anything like it before Maybe it isn't an animal from the woods; could it really be some sort of monster? She's desperate for someone else to see it to confirm her suspicion, to confirm that she isn't going crazy.

The way we have it now, she runs back to Sophie's house even though she's basically in the driveway of her own house. So you might want her to run back to Sophie's house deliberately, with the monster chasing her, so that Sophie can confirm that this is no ordinary animal. (We'd have to come up with a reason why she just doesn't go into her own house and look for one of her parents to do this. Because this is another problem with this scene: There's ample time for her to run into the safety of her own house when the monster is licking the squirrel. You'll need to take another look at this and tinker with it.)

Monster Reveal: When Arnie turns into the monster at the birthday party, Amy doesn't acknowledge that he's the monster she's been seeing. THIS IS NOT BELIEVABLE! The story CAN'T unfold this way. There is no way that she wouldn't realize this is her monster(!) and seek vindication from Lissa and her parents who mocked her. She didn't imagine it! The monster is real! She's relieved. What's unreal is that it's her brother.

When she is recovering at home, she never asks her

parents anything about this monster—did you KNOW he was a monster? Etc. AND THE PARENTS NEVER REACT TO THE FACT THAT THEIR SON HAS JUST TURNED INTO A MONSTER. They act as if this is perfectly normal. THIS TOO IS UNBELIEVABLE. Amy doesn't question why they aren't shocked. And all the parents do is wonder how they can turn him back to Arnie.

I know you wanted the reveal – that Arnie is the monster she's been seeing-- to come as a surprise to the reader later, but that simply won't work. It's obvious that it's him. It's obvious to the readers and it would be obvious to Amy. All the reactions you have in this scene—Amy's and the parents'—are illogical and unbelievable. (By the way, Lissa comes in and she doesn't act very surprised either.)

Here is an easy fix: If you want some sort of surprise later, you can have the parents lie here to Amy. "OMG, your brother has turned into a monster. This is unbelievable! How could this have happened? It must have been something in the slime.

Amy can protest. She can say it wasn't her fault. She's been trying to tell them--he was a monster before the slime. But they say they don't believe this. It was definitely the slime, they say. Amy is so frustrated! She thought she'd be vindicated, but they still don't believe her.

Then, the surprise reveal later is that they knew all along

about Arnie but didn't tell her. They adopted him because they felt sorry for him. No one else wanted him. And they thought if he lived with people, he would change, become more human. But now the slime did something to him. In the past, he could always change back after a few minutes. But it's probably the glue. The glue made him stick this way...

Amy's reaction to discovering the animal is a monster:

After animal/monster encounter in her driveway, Amy doesn't think anymore about the beast. She doesn't think about it in the video store, the smoothie shop, while baking the cake, etc. She never looks over her shoulder when she's outside. She never worries about it coming after her again.

Instead, she should be very nervous about it. And she should be devising a plan to lure the monster out so she can prove to everyone that it really exists, that she didn't make it up.

Maybe you can add a scene where she leaves some pizza outside to attract it . She checks the trap; the pizza is gone. Yes! She's very excited! She follows the animal prints—and finds a raccoon family on a pizza picnic. If you can add a scene or two like this and add the Amy interstitials where she's addressing the reader, you'll be able to cut some of the bad behavior events up front that don't quite work and keep the page count.

The End: Amy should come up with the idea of getting the smoothies. She doesn't do much in this book; she mostly complains, so it would be good to have her solve the problem. She can send Lissa to the store but still keep it a secret from the reader until Lissa appears with the drink. (See notes on manuscript for this.)

There are other notes on the manuscript that discuss issues beyond these, but these are the heftier ones. Still, I think you should look through the notes before you start revising.

Hope you find this helpful, dude.

Your pal,
SL

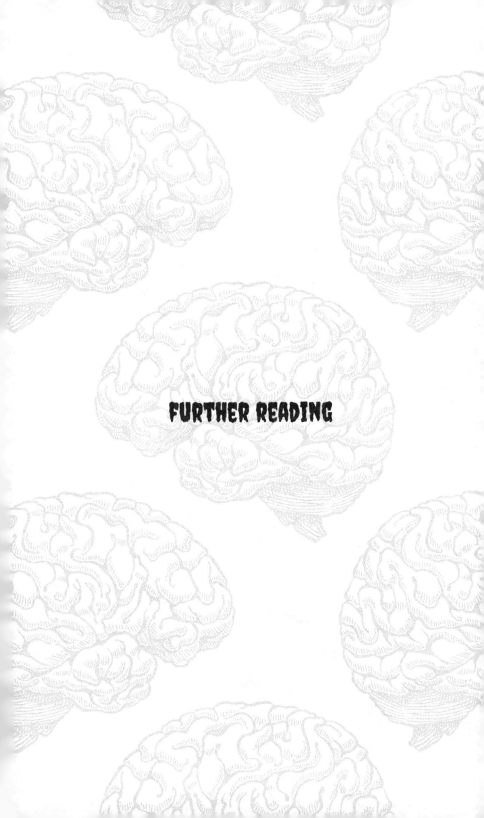

FURTHER READING

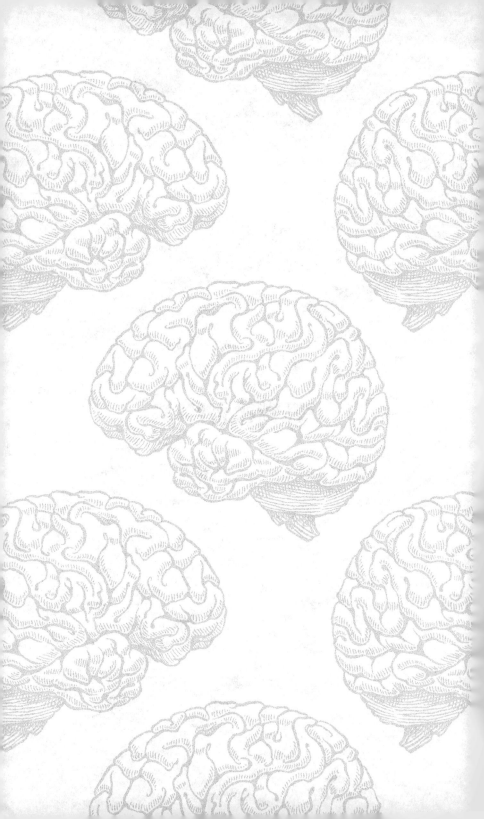

R.L. STINE'S 50 FAVORITE BOOKS

1. P.G. Wodehouse, *Right Ho, Jeeves,* Herbert Jenkins, 1934
2. P.G. Wodehouse, *Uncle Fred in the Springtime,* Doubleday, 1939
3. P.G. Wodehouse, *Summer Lightning,* Herbert Jenkins, 1929
4. Ray Bradbury, *Dandelion Wine,* Doubleday, 1957
5. Ray Bradbury, *Something Wicked This Way Comes,* Simon & Schuster, 1962
6. Garrison Keillor, *Liberty: A Lake Wobegon Novel,* Viking, 2008
7. Robert Sheckley, *Mindswap,* Orb Books, 2006
8. Robert Klane, *Where's Poppa?,* Random House, 1970
9. Joseph Heller, *Catch-22,* Simon & Schuster, 1961
10. Georges Simenon, *Maigret and the Mad Woman,* Presses de la Cité, 1970
11. Georges Simenon, *Maigret and the Headless Corpse,* Presses de la Cité, 1955
12. Agatha Christie, *Sparkling Cyanide,* Dodd, Mead, and Company, 1945
13. Agatha Christie, *The ABC Murders,* Collins Crime Hub, 1936
14. Ruth Rendell, *Master of the Moor,* Pantheon Books, 1982
15. Ira Levin, *A Kiss Before Dying,* Simon & Schuster, 1953
16. Robert B. Parker, *Paper Doll,* Putnam, 1993

17. Robert B. Parker, *Cold Service,* Putnam, 2005

18. Harlan Coben, *Drop Shot,* Dell, 1996

19. Harlan Coben, *Tell No One,* Dell, 2009

20. Lee Child, *Killing Floor,* Putnam, 1997

21. Michael Connelly, *The Lincoln Lawyer,* Little, Brown, and Company, 2005

22. Mark Twain, *Adventures of Huckleberry Finn,* Charles L. Webster and Company, 1885

23. Gabriel García Márquez, *One Hundred Years of Solitude,* Harper & Row, 1967

24. Max Shulman, *Barefoot Boy With Cheek,* Bantam, 1959

25. Woody Allen, *Without Feathers,* Random House, 1975

26. Laurence Sterne, *The Life and Opinions of Tristram Shandy, Gentleman,* Ann Ward (vol. 1–2), Dodsley (vol. 3–4), Becket & DeHondt (vol. 5–9), 1759–1767

27. Amy Tan, *The Kitchen God's Wife,* Putnam, 1991

28. Edith Wharton, *The House of Mirth,* Scribner, 1905

29. Anthony Trollope, *The Way We Live Now,* Champan and Hall, 1875

30. Charles Dickens, *The Life and Adventures of Martin Chuzzlewit,* Champan and Hall, 1844

31. Frank Capra, *The Name Above the Title: An Autobiography,* Vintage, 1971

32. Harpo Marx, *Harpo Speaks!,* Bernard Geis Associates, 1961

33. Erik Larson, *The Devil in the White City,* Crown, 2003

34. Art Spiegelman, *Maus*, Pantheon Books, 1991

35. John Updike, The Rabbit novels, Alfred A. Knopf, 1960–2001

36. Sebastian Barry, *A Long Long Way*, Viking, 2005

37. Vladimir Nabokov, *Lolita*, Olympia Press, 1955

38. Vladimir Nabokov, *Pale Fire*, Putnam, 1962

39. John le Carré, *Tinker Tailor Soldier Spy*, Random House, 1974

40. Brian Selznick, *The Marvels*, Scholastic, 2015

41. Kazuo Ishiguro, *Never Let Me Go*, Faber and Faber, 2005

42. Keigo Higashino, *The Devotion of Suspect X*, Minotaur Books, 2012

43. James Clavell, *Shōgun*, Delacorte, 1975

44. Stephen King, *Misery*, Viking, 1987

45. Stephen King, *The Shining*, Doubleday, 1977

46. Carter Dickson, *The Judas Window*, Morrow, 1938

47. John Dickson Carr, *The Three Coffins*, Harper, 1935

48. Raymond Chandler, *The High Window*, Alfred A. Knopf, 1942

49. Joe Keenan, *Blue Heaven*, Penguin Books, 1988

50. Peter Lovesey, *The False Inspector Dew*, Macmillan, 1982

RL STINE BOOKS: SUGGESTED READING

- *Give Me a K - I - L - L,* St. Martin's Press, 2017
- *I Am Slappy's Evil Twin,* Scholastic, 2017
- *It Came From Beneath the Sink!,* Scholastic, 1995
- *Missing,* Pocket Books, 1990
- *One Day at HorrorLand,* Scholastic, 1994
- *The Curse of the Mummy's Tomb,* Scholastic, 1993
- *Revenge of the Lawn Gnomes,* Scholastic, 1995
- *Say Cheese and Die!,* Scholastic, 1992
- *Little Shop of Hamsters,* Scholastic, 2010
- *Welcome to Camp Nightmare,* Scholastic, 1993
- *Attack of the Mutant,* Scholastic, 1993
- *The Haunted Mask,* Scholastic, 1993
- *The Girl Who Cried Monster,* Scholastic, 1993
- *How I Met My Monster,* Scholastic, 2013
- *Frankenstein's Dog,* Scholastic, 2013
- *Deep Trouble,* Scholastic, 1994
- *Young Scrooge,* Square Fish, 2017
- *My Hairiest Adventure,* Scholastic, 1994
- *The Scarecrow Walks at Midnight,* Scholastic, 1994

OTHER NOTABLE BOOKS

- Julia Cameron, *The Artist's Way*, Penguin Group, 1992
- Aristotle, Poetics
- Deborah and James Howe, *Bunnicula*, Atheneum Books, 1979
- Suzanne Collins, *The Hunger Games*, Scholastic, 2008
- Brandilyn Collins, *Getting Into Character: Seven Secrets a Novelist Can Learn From Actors*, Wiley, 2002
- Lynda Barry, *Syllabus: Notes From an Accidental Professor*, Drawn and Quarterly, 2014
- J.D. Salinger, *The Catcher in the Rye*, Little, Brown, 1951
- Agatha Christie, *Sparkling Cyanide*, Dodd, Mead, and Company, 1945
- Ray Bradbury, *Something Wicked This Way Comes*, Simon & Schuster, 1962
- Stephen King, *Pet Sematary*, Doubleday, 1983
- Stephen King, *On Writing: A Memoir of the Craft*, Scribner, 2000
- Robert B. Parker, *The Godwulf Manuscript*,
- Houghton Mifflin, 1973
- Robert Crais, *The Forgotten Man*, Ballantine, 2005
- S.E. Hinton, *The Outsiders*, Viking Press, Dell Publishing, 1967
- Mark Shatz and Mel Hilitzer, *Comedy Writing Secrets: The*

Bestselling Guide to Writing (3rd Edition), Writer's Digest Books, 1987

- Anne Lamott, *Bird by Bird: Some Instructions on Writing and Life,* Pantheon, 1994
- William Strunk Jr. and E.B. White, *The Elements of Style,* Harcourt, Brace & Howe, 1920
- P.G. Wodehouse, *Thank You, Jeeves,* Herbert Jenkins, 1934

ABOUT THE AUTHOR

R.L. Stine is one of the best-selling children's authors in history. Goosebumps, which recently celebrated its 30th anniversary, has more than 400 million books in print in 32 languages. An all-new Goosebumps series, House of Shivers, will debut in September 2023.

The Goosebumps series made R.L. Stine a worldwide publishing celebrity (and Jeopardy answer). His other popular children's book series include *Fear Street*, (recently revived as a feature film trilogy), *The Garbage Pail Kids*, *Mostly Ghostly*, *The Nightmare Room*, and *Rotten School*. Other titles include: *It's The First Day of School Forever*, *A Midsummer Night's Scream*, *Young Scrooge*, *Stinetinglers*, and three picture books, with Marc Brown—*The Little Shop of Monsters*, *Mary McScary*, and *Why Did the Monster Cross the Road* (July 4, 2023).

The Goosebumps TV series was the number-one

children's show in America for three years. The episodes can still be seen on Netflix. More recently, R.L.'s anthology TV series, *R.L. Stine's The Haunting Hour,* won the Emmy Award three years in a row as Best Children›s Show. His newest Disney+ TV series is *Just Beyond,* based on his graphic novels for BOOM! Studios. Two Goosebumps feature films starring Jack Black as R.L. Stine were released in 2015 and 2018. The first film became the #1 film in America. The *Fear Street* movies all reached #1 on Netflix.

RL. Stine lives in New York City with his wife Jane, an editor and publisher. You can connect with him on Twitter @RL_Stine, as well as on Instagram and Facebook. For more information, visit rlstine.com.

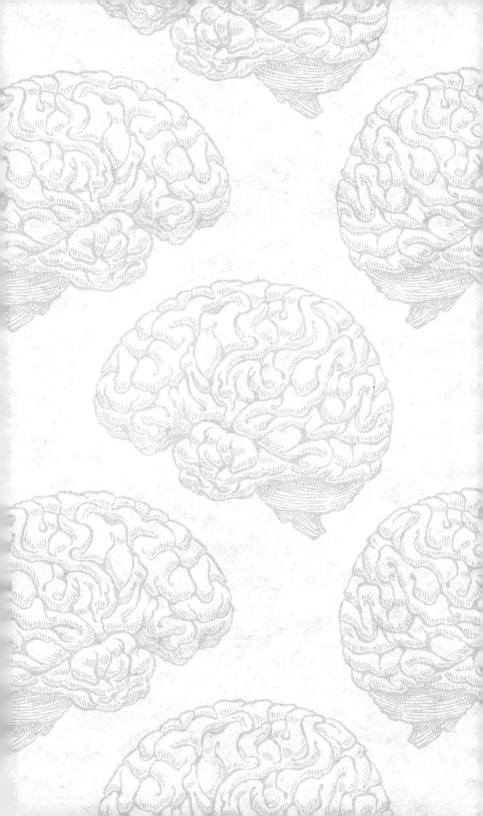

NOTE FROM THE PUBLISHER

This book is a culmination of ambition and vision, but not necessarily for the author — in fact, Mr. Stine was reluctant to embark on this endeavor at the beginning.

Nestled within our distribution warehouse in Twin Falls, Idaho, Di Angelo Publications has an office with chalkboard walls. For many years, one of these walls has contained a list of names, with the words "Sequoia's Hit List" scribbled on top. This hit list, personally built by both myself and my staff, is full of our dream authors — people who we would be honored to work alongside in publishing their books. Some have never written a book, and some are legends in the literary space.

For as long as this list has existed, there has been a single name that remained at the top: R.L. Stine.

My stalking started many years ago, first through emails (to an address I later found out was incorrect), then through messages on Instagram. Fortunately, Mr. Stine is tech savvy and caught up with the modern times of social media — he even manages his own account! Over the course of a year and a half, Mr. Stine received a series of messages from me — not just written, but videos as well. I would check in with him on a weekly basis, introducing him to my staff, showing him around our warehouse, and constantly encouraging him to give us an opportunity to work together. His continuous polite declines only fueled me further in my mission to work with the great horror writer.

In June of 2022, Di Angelo Publications had a publishing booth at the ALA (American Library Association) show in Washington, D.C., where I knew Mr. Stine would be a guest speaker. I stood eagerly in the longest line of the show with all the other fans, waiting for a face-to-face with R.L. Stine. One by one, he signed the participants' books. Courteously and professionally, he would look up for a photo with a fan, before quickly returning to his signing. As the fans placed their books in front of him, I knew my turn was coming . . . but as everyone else slid a "Goosebumps" or "Fear Street" on the table, I slid a piece of paper with the words "Publishing Contract" and a signature line. Just as Stine was about to sign, he paused — then looked up, saw my face, and burst out into laughter. That was the moment I knew we would be fast friends.

It was not until months later that I was in NYC and

invited him to lunch. It was at this very lunch that Mr. Stine divulged his secret love for banana cream pies. Little did he realize, following his proclamation of love, banana cream pies would be continuously delivered to his front door. Months later (with the help of my pie bribe), Mr. Stine would finally consider accepting my offer to make a book together. The acceptance, however, came on the condition that I would have to get Masterclass' approval if we were to use his fiction writing as a basis for the nonfiction book.

Following our conversation with Masterclass, the book started to come together fast. We shot the cover in early April of 2023 and worked through the editorial process to prepare the book for production.

This endeavor has been one of the highlights of my career. It is rare to find that an international treasure, such as Mr. Stine, is also a genuine person who is willing to give opportunity to new ideas. The honor of working with R.L. Stine will forever be embedded in the hearts and minds of the DAP team, and in the pages of this book.

—Sequoia
Founder of Di Angelo Publications

Erudition

ABOUT THE PUBLISHER

Di Angelo Publications was founded in 2008 by Sequoia Schmidt—at the age of seventeen. The modernized publishing firm's creative headquarters is in Los Angeles, California, with its distribution center located in Twin Falls, Idaho. In 2020, Di Angelo Publications made a conscious decision to move all printing and production for domestic distribution of its books to the United States. The firm is comprised of eleven imprints, and the featured imprint, Erudition, was inspired by the desire to spread knowledge, spark curiosity, and add numbers to the ranks of continuing learners, big and small.

DAP BOOKS
DI ANGELO PUBLICATIONS